Jan Glazewski

BLOOD AND SILVER

*A true story of survival and
a son's search for his family treasure*

Tafelberg

Tafelberg, an imprint of NB Publishers,
a division of Media24 Books Pty (Ltd),
40 Heerengracht, Cape Town, South Africa
www.tafelberg.com

Text © 2022 Jan Glazewski
Photographs © The Glazewski-Edwards family

All rights reserved.
No part of this book may be reproduced or transmitted in any form
or by any electronic or mechanical means, including photocopying
and recording, or by any other information storage or retrieval
system, without written permission from the publisher.

Set in 11,5 on 16 pt Linux Libertine
Edited by Russell Martin
Cover design by Stephen Symons
Book design by Nazli Jacobs
Printed and bound by CTP Printers, Cape Town

First edition, first impression 2022

ISBN: 978-0-624-09369-5
Epub: 978-0-624-09370-1

To my late father, Gustaw,
who provided not only a map to guide me to the treasure
but also an example of how to meet the
challenges presented by life.

There is no such thing as a coincidence.
— *Anonymous*

CONTENTS

Prologue	11
A Note on Names and Pronunciation	16
Author's Note	17
Acknowledgements	18
Map: Poland before and after World War II	19
PART 1: EARLY DAYS	**21**
Chapter 1 My Bloody Beginnings	23
Chapter 2 A Farm Called Cotswold	38
Chapter 3 Vygeboom Days	48
PART 2: LIFEBOATS	**61**
Chapter 4 Education, Education, Education	63
Chapter 5 My Blossoming Career	75
Chapter 6 Four Years to Live	85
Chapter 7 Living and Working with HIV	101
Chapter 8 Entering Ukraine	120
Chapter 9 Finding Louise	137
PART 3: FINDING SILVER ... AND GOLD	**143**
Chapter 10 The Silver Beckons	145
Chapter 11 Silverware in Sight	164
Chapter 12 Dark Clouds, Silver Linings	189
Epilogue	199
Layla's diary	211
About the author	223

PROLOGUE

A Treasure Map

*On the border of the forest... among the trees... you must look for
our silver and my hunting guns.*
– Instruction accompanying my father's treasure map

AFTER SUPPER one evening, on one of my monthly visits to my parents' home in Durbanville, Cape Town, my father and I retreated to his study where he customarily sat at his roll-top desk while my stepmother, Kathleen, tidied up after our meal. Here he gave me a hand-drawn map and instructions as to the whereabouts of the family treasure, whose buried existence I had heard about since childhood. Possibly because his handwriting was indecipherable, he had typed the instructions, using the old Olivetti typewriter I remember from my childhood with its faded letter 'a'. The document, dated 4 September 1989, directed me to the treasure buried in September 1939, somewhere in a forest adjoining my late grandfather's former estate called Chmielowa in Eastern Europe.

The instructions are headed 'Route to Chmielowa'. The estate was situated on the banks of the Dniester River, which runs along the foothills of the Carpathian mountains. Prior to World War II, when my father was a young man recently wed to my mother, the area was located in eastern Poland near the border with Russia. Immediately after the war, with the realignment of borders at Yalta, the farm became part of the Union of Soviet Socialist Republics (USSR) and was subject to communist rule behind the Iron Curtain. In the early 1990s, nearly fifty years later, communism fell and the Soviet Union broke up into several independent countries, including Ukraine. Thus, while my father had buried the treasure in Poland, by the time I got to think about recovering it, it was in Ukraine, which, despite the overthrow of the communist regime, reeked of the former bureaucratic regime for at least a decade. My father's home town, Lwów as he knew it, but now Lviv, and my grandfather's estate are now situated in Ukraine.

Remarkably, my father drew the map and wrote the accompanying instructions from memory, some fifty years after he left former Poland with my mother at the onset of the war. His instructions culminate in a reference to the pencil-drawn map and the following directive: 'On the left side of the pencil-drawn map you will see the broken line going from the stone wall towards the forest (oaks) it is there on the border of the forest but already among the trees that you must look for our silver and my hunting guns.'

In 1989, the year my father gave me the map, apartheid South Africa was in a second State of Emergency, which had been declared three years previously by President PW Botha during an era of intense political turmoil. I was preoccupied with these events as well as with making a mark in my new position on the academic staff at the University of Cape Town (UCT), so I simply put the documents away in an old box file in my study marked 'Poland'. It was a decade later, after my father's death, that I hauled them out of their dusty storage place. On reading the last phrase that I 'must look for our silver and my hunting guns', I, for some inexplicable reason, let out a deep-seated wail. It seemed that there was some important message here, but it was only subsequently that I was to understand its import.

The period during which South Africa underwent political upheaval saw the rise in Poland of Solidarity, a trade union movement led by Lech Wałęsa, which led to the downfall of communism in Poland and, eventually, other Eastern bloc countries. Thus, both the country of my birth, South Africa, and the country of my forebears, Poland, attained freedom from their political oppressors at more or less the same time.

A Treasure Map

In Poland, a Solidarity-led coalition government was formed and Wałęsa was elected president in 1990 – the same year that the African National Congress (ANC) was unbanned and Nelson Mandela was released from prison. At that time I had recently taken up a position at UCT's Institute of Marine Law (later, the Institute of Marine and Environmental Law).

Although the map and instructions were given to me by my father when I was adult, I had heard about the buried treasure as a child. I don't recollect the first time that it was mentioned by *Tatuś*, but I must have been less than ten years old when the hope of finding it was first instilled in me. But before the search could even begin, there were a few hurdles for me to leap over...

My father's map:

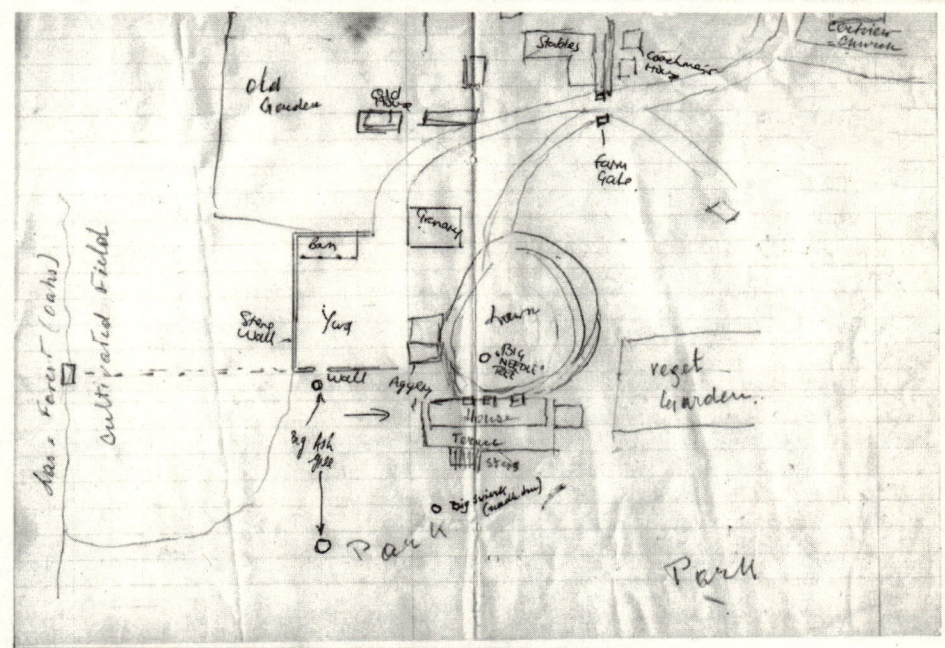

13

PROLOGUE

My father's instructions dated September 1989:

4th Sept.1989

THE ROUTE TO CHMIELOWA.

To reach CHMIELOWA from present Poland, you must first reach LWOW, which is at present in Russia in Western Ukraine. From Franek Rozwadowski's relation (he was in Lwow in Oct.1986) there is no air communication at present from Poland direct to Lwow. From Poland all planes are going to Moskow. From there you might get a plane to Lwow or to Kiew (the capital of Western Ukraine). From Warsaw there is a plane to Rzeszów, which is a town between Krakow an Lwow. So from Poland you can go to Lwów either by train : Kraków — Rzeszów — Lwów, or by plane from Warsaw to Rzeszów and further by train to Lwów. By train you go from Rzeszów through Przemyśl-Łańcut to Lwów. According to Franio in Przemyśl one goes through Polish passport and custum control, and one has to change the train from polish (the same as European) rail width to Russian (wider) rail width. The coaches are also different with the wheels wider apart then European or Polish coaches. The first station on the russian side of the frontier is Mościska where one goes through Russian passport and custum control. On the Russian side of the frontier you change yuor watches two hours back. Franek & annemarie R. stayed in Lwów in hotel which was called "George" in my days and now is an "Intourist" hotel on before the war "Marjacki" square (our Lady) now "Mickiewicza" square.

Once in Lwów you might be interested to see the house during my school days. Nabielaka No 1 from 1917 up to 1925 when we moved into villa "Romana" which my father bought on Potockiego No 55 opposite the church of Karmelitan Sisters. From that villa Romana i was going to my VIII (eighths) gimnazium which was first on the corner of Czarneckiego and Łyczakowska streets but I matriculated in the new building on Dwernickiego str, in 1926. I started to farm in Chmielowa in November 1929 and my father sold villa Romana in 1933 and joined me in Chmielowa.

Let's now concentrate on how to reach Cmielowa. From Lwowyou can go to Chmielowa either by train or by road. From Lwów I was normally taking a train from the Main Station a train international with the destination Bucrest a/ in Rumania.

You had to change the train in Stanisławów where you had to take the train going to Buczacz and further to Czortków. From that train you had to get out either in Buczacz, or better one station further at Pyszkowce. I remember the distance marked on the railway tickets from Lwów to Pyszkowce via Stanisławów was 236km. From Pyszkowce by road to Chmielowa was another 26 km via Jazłowiec. Jazłowiec was my Post Office and telephone exchange 12 km from Chmielowa. From what I remember it was a shorter distance from Lwów to Chmielowa by road then by train, because by road one avoided the detour to Stanisławów. If one goes from Lwów to Chmielowa by road one has to leave Lwów by Łyczakowska gate towards Brzeżany — Podhajce — Monasterzyska to Buchach (all four towns are marked on the big, framed map, the enlargement of the photograph of the pre-first world-war military austrian map.

A Treasure Map

Once you arrived by train to Buczacz or Pyszkowce, or by road to Buczacz you take the road towards Jazłowiec + about 15 km from Buczacz. Jazłowiec was my Post Office and my telefone Exchange, Chmielowa was No 14, Jazlowiec is situated deep in a valey, you claimb the main road from Jazłowiec, pass on your right the Convent of the Sisters of Immaculate Conception with a sharp bend to the left. Follow the main road and turn off to the right about 2-3km from the Convent towards Beremiany or Swierzkowce, but instead turning to the right again towards those villages you carry on straight another couple of kilometers go throgh a small valey and then turn to the right towards Chmielowa. Just before you reach the village you passe village cemetry on your right, carry on straight passing on your left the Cerkiew (greko-catholic church) and if you still caary on strait few hundred meters after passing the cerkiew you enter the gate of the folwark (farm buildings) Chmielowa. (see pencil drawn map). On the enlargements of the map you fill find two Chmielowas, dont confuse our Chmielowa with the one on the other side of the river Dniester which has nothing to do with us. On the left side of the pencil drawn map you will see the broken line going from the stone wall towards the forest (oaks) it is there on the border of the forest but already among the trees that you must look for our silver and my hunting guns.

A Note on Names and Pronunciation

PLACE NAMES

The names Lviv and Lwów are used interchangeably in this book, as they refer to the same town. It was here that my father grew up and went to school, and where my grandfather had his business. In general, I use Lviv when referring to present-day events as the town now forms part of Ukraine; in referring to the past, I have chosen the interwar usage, Lwów, as the town was known while still part of Poland. Prior to World War I and throughout the nineteenth century, the town was known as Lemberg, when it was part of the Austro-Hungarian Empire. It became Lvov after World War II, when it was incorporated into the Union of Soviet Socialist Republics. In 1991, after the dissolution of the USSR, it became Lviv, and is today in Ukraine. Similarly, I use the pre-World War II name Żółkiew (now Zhovka) when I describe my trip to that village in Ukraine.

POLISH PERSONAL NAMES
(*Pronunciation key*: *a* as in cat; *e* as in bed; *ee* as in meet; *i* as in pin; *o* as in top; *oo* as in soon; *uh* as in along; *ch* as in church; *f* as in fat; *j* as in jam; *kh* as in loch; *ng* as in French vin; *v* as in van; *w* as in will; *y* as in yes; *zh* as in vision)

Ciocia [**cho**-cha]: Aunt (blood relative); also a term of respect for an older woman who is a close family friend
Dziadzio [**jya**-jyo]: Grandpa
Pan: Mr
Pani: Mrs
Strij [striy]: Uncle (one's father's brother)

Tatuś [ta-toosh]: Daddy (as opposed to more formal *ojciec* denoting father)

Wuj [vooy]: Uncle (one's mother's brother); also a term of respect for a family friend

The feminine form of a surname has the suffix '-ska', so Glazewski (male), Glazewska (female)

Pronunciation of some Polish names appearing in the book
Andrzej — an-jey
Chmielowa — khmye-loh-vuh
Cieński — tsi-eng-ski
Ewa — ev-uh
Glazewski — gluh-zef-ski
Gustaw — goos-tav
Ignacy — ig-na-si
Jabłońska — ya-bwong-skuh
Kazimierz — ka-zi-myerzh
Lwów — lvoof
Łyczakowski — wich-uh-kof-ski
Paweł — pa-vew
Puzyna, Tychna — pyoo-zi-nuh, tikh-nuh
Taras — ta-ras
Tysson — tis-son
Wrocław — vrot-swaf
Zaleszczyki — za-lesh-chi-ki
Zbigniew — zbig-nyef
Żółkiew — zhoow-kyef

Author's Note

Some names have been changed to protect individuals involved.

Acknowledgements

To the late Anne Schuster and her creative writing classes (where I enjoyed being the only male in the group);

Liz Mackenzie, who taught me to write what I mean;

My editors, Lynda Gilfillan and Russell Martin, for their incisive suggestions and meticulous editing;

Erika Oosthuysen, of NB Publishers, for her enthusiastic adoption of the project;

Gordon McIntyre, Trevor McGlashan, Maniunia Spence, Don Pinnock, Lana Kenney, Michael and Helena Janisch and Dana Francis, who contributed to the work in different ways;

My nomad niece Layla, without whom her 'nutty uncle' would not have found the treasure;

And, lastly, my wife, Louise, for her love and support:

My grateful thanks are due.

The publisher and author gratefully acknowledge the permission granted to reproduce four lines from the poem by Adam Zagajewski, 'Jechać do Lwowa', translated into English by Renata Gorczynski (https://www.poetryfoundation.org/poems/48313/to-go-to-lvo).

Poland before and after World War II

Note: The highlighted line depicts current-day Poland. The part of current-day Poland to the west of the dotted line indicates the territory ceded to Poland after World War II at Yalta in 1945. The territories to the east of the current eastern border of Poland are the parts of pre-World War II Poland that were ceded to the USSR in 1945; they now form parts of Ukraine, Lithuania and Belarus.

PART 1

Early Days

CHAPTER 1

My Bloody Beginnings

MY HEALTH-related problems began at birth in 1953.

'He must be circumcised,' announced the white-coated doctor in an Afrikaans accent in the maternity ward at Paarl Hospital. Paarl is a small rural town about half an hour's drive from Cape Town.

I was a few days old.

'No, please no!' pleaded my gaunt father in his thick Polish accent. 'He will bleed! He has just been diagnosed as a haemophiliac. His brother died as baby of internal bleeding.'

At the time, my father was managing the farm L'Ormarins in the Franschhoek valley. While today it is a prestigious wine estate owned by the Rupert family, then it was a regular fruit farm owned by Count Ludek Cieński, who was part of the Polish diaspora that arrived in South Africa after World War II.

I imagine that my father's memory would have leapt back in time, from Paarl to Palestine and to memories of Adam, his first-born son, named after my grandfather, and also a haemophiliac. My parents had noticed that, from birth, Adam seemed to bleed more profusely than normal, and that he bruised easily. He died tragically young.

My mother could not bear the prospect of her second son also bleeding to death and retreated to the cold hospital corridor in her white towelling dressing gown. Too anguished to speak, she also battled with English, let alone Afrikaans, in this alien land, so different and remote from her richly textured life in rural Poland. Now, as an adult, I often wonder how baby Adam's death and the realisation that she was the carrier of the haemophilia gene affected her.

'Ja-nee, vitamin K will do the trick,' announced the doctor confidently. 'A new treatment *vir hierdie tipe* bleeding disorder. It will stop any bleeding, straight. We must go ahead and circumcise him.'

But vitamin K is not used to treat haemophilia: it is used to treat a related bleeding disorder. As a result, they went ahead with the procedure, and I bled profusely. Incisions had to be made in my six-day-old ankles, with plastic tubes inserted into the veins so that I could receive life-saving blood. Over sixty years later, I still bear the scars. Although I bled and bled, I clearly had a strong internal desire to live, refusing to go the way of my brother. So began my battle with haemophilia, a genetic blood disorder caused by a lack of clotting factor. This results in both external and internal bleeding, the latter causing the blood to damage the smooth part of the joints and leading to severe damage and pain over time.

*

I was born more than a decade after Adam died, yet he seems always to have been in my bones. I once went to an esoteric healer, who called herself 'the Angel Lady', to get advice on my health and related issues. As I was recounting to her that I had three sisters, numerous step-siblings, a half-brother and a half-sister, she interjected, 'No, I sense another presence, do you not have a brother?'

Many years after my father's death, I found Adam's death certificate among his papers. Written in Latin, it had been issued by a Catholic church in Rehovot. I resolved that, before I died, I would search for Adam's grave in that city, which is in today's Israel. It turned out that such a visit was not necessary, as in an extraordinary turn of events someone I once befriended on a cruise to Antarctica later located his grave while on a visit to Israel and sent me eight treasured photographs of the site.

*

Haemophilia is a rare hereditary disease which mostly affects males. It has been dubbed the 'royal disease' as it was prevalent among the aristocratic families of Europe during the late eighteenth and early nineteenth centuries. Queen Victoria was a carrier of the disease. Not only was her son Leopold affected, but two of her daughters as well as her granddaughter Alexandra became carriers. As is well known, Alexandra became the tsarina of Russia, having married Tsar Nicholas II. Their son, Alexei, a haemophiliac who was treated by the notorious Rasputin, was next in line to the throne, but the entire family was assassinated by the Bolsheviks in 1918. Whenever the topic of my haemophilia comes up at dinner parties, I jokingly say that my great-grandmother was a chambermaid in the tsar's palace. In reality, it would have been impossible for me to have contracted haemophilia that way, as it was the tsarina Alexandra who was a carrier. This fact seems to get overlooked when I tell the story.

There are gradations of the disease – mild, moderate, and severe – depending on how much factor VIII (the blood-clotting factor) the liver produces. In my case, it is zero. Being a severe haemophiliac, I bruise easily and bleed profusely if I cut myself. When I went through the usual childhood process of losing my milk teeth, I left pillowcases covered in blood, much to the distress of my mother, who was ill at the time.

The most difficult aspect of my condition has been the internal bleeding into my joints, in particular my ankles, knees and elbows. This was the result of physical activity such as kicking balls during my youth, walking down mountain tracks, digging in the garden, carrying heavy bags, hitting golf balls and more. The internal bleeding and resultant joint damage cause extreme pain, which gets worse over time, particularly if not treated with factor VIII, my blood product. My gait once prompted my friend's five-year-old daughter to ask, 'Why does that man walk so softly, Dad?'

Since turning forty I have had both my knees replaced, my left ankle fused, and, straight after retiring, my right ankle replaced. I'm now in my late sixties and in 2021, despite Covid-19 restrictions, have also had my left elbow replaced. It occurs to me that eventually I may have to have my head replaced as well. I am, consequently, a problem case when going through airport security.

One of my earliest memories is of standing on the stoep at our home on Cotswold farm near Durbanville. I had dropped a glass bottle and cut my big toe. Blood was flowing everywhere. I am told that I was rushed to Groote Schuur Hospital in Cape Town. This was a major undertaking for my parents as Cotswold, the farm that my father was then renting, was some distance from the city and my father's car was a clapped-out Standard Vanguard, which was not sure to manage the trip. This was the first of many spells that I spent in hospital, from childhood through to my teenage years.

On another occasion, I was eight or nine years old and trying to learn to ride a bicycle. It belonged to one of the Inglis boys, who lived across a field from the house we occupied after my father remarried. Together with two of my newly acquired stepbrothers, John and Martin, I spent endless hours at the Inglis household during the school holidays, mucking about with two of their four sons, William and Paul. Their vast lawn made for a good cricket field, and we often played there while their parents watched from the balcony, having a customary cup of tea with biscuits. But I was trying to learn to ride William's bicycle, and the other boys had gone off somewhere…

I am struggling. I seat myself on the bike, put my right foot gingerly on the ground, hoist myself up, and push the pedal with my left foot. But I slip and hit my groin on the crossbar. I try again and again, but the same thing happens. The bike is too big for me. But I persist and eventually get it right. I ride a triumphant full circle around the lawn without falling. Soon after, I hear the old slave bell that hangs on our back stoep. It tolls for us three boys, a signal to return home to weigh and pack my father's battery chickens and help with the rest of the evening routine.

Next morning, I wake up feeling uncomfortable in my groin area. I gingerly lift my sheet and see that my scrotum is purple and blue and as large as a tennis ball. I alert John and Martin, with whom I share a bedroom. One of them runs downstairs. My stepmother arrives, lifts the sheet with some embarrassment, takes one look, and drops it immediately. 'Oh my goodness! We have to take you to hospital.' So, once again, off to Groote Schuur I go.

A later memory is of a visit to the local dentist in Durbanville village, again with John and Martin. When the injection hit a vein, my entire jaw and cheekbone swelled up instantly. My father signed the consent paper for me to undergo a tracheotomy as my breathing was compromised, but fortunately the swelling subsided after the first transfusion of the vital clotting factor. I was told afterwards that a Mass was said at our local Catholic church, praying for my recovery. This clearly did the trick.

I recollect sitting for endless hours on hospital benches as a teenager. On one occasion I was admonished by a doctor for reading my own hospital folder. 'But whose body is this anyway?' I asked myself.

*

During my growing-up years I would often have to be admitted to hospital to have blood transfusions to stem internal or external bleeding, sometimes for up to two weeks. But with medical advances over time it was discovered that haemophiliacs need only a tiny constituent of whole blood. Since the mid-1970s, we can have our clotting factor, extracted from whole blood, close at hand. We can then inject ourselves when necessary or prophylactically once or twice a week. This has been a life-changer for sufferers by obviating the need for protracted stays in hospital and waiting in the casualty section for essential treatment.

On one occasion, when I was about ten, I was lying in bed at Groote Schuur Hospital soon after the doctor had put the daily drip up next to my bed and left for her rounds. My chest tightened, and I struggled to breathe. I hoarsely called out to the nurse hurrying past, but she was too preoccupied to pay attention. This is it, I thought, and resigned myself to the fact that I might be facing death. But just then my white-coated stepbrother, Peter, appeared. He was a medical student at the time and had fortuitously popped in at that moment to see how I was doing. He immediately called the medics, who recognised an allergic reaction. I felt relief the moment the antihistamine was injected.

The beauty of the new clotting factor treatment is that haemophiliacs can inject themselves with the equivalent of eight or more people's blood donations in one small, concentrated dose. But that brings with it an increased risk of receiving blood products that are contaminated, for example with hepatitis B, hepatitis C and, more devastatingly, the human immunodeficiency virus (HIV) virus that emerged in the mid-1980s. HIV affected haemophiliacs worldwide, including me, as I later relate. Ironically, being a privileged white South African exposed me to greater risk than my black haemophiliac compatriots. I had access to the more expensive, imported concentrate factor, while they were on the home-produced cryoprecipitate. For them, the risk of contamination was negligible because HIV was still extremely rare in South Africa.

Over the past decade or two, further technological advances have been made. Factor VIII can be manufactured artificially, ensuring that no contaminants are transfused. Most significantly, with new gene therapy, trials are being conducted on the possibility of haemophilia being cured – at least in some patients. But that was not part of my story.

*

My Polish refugee parents and their three young daughters had arrived in South Africa in 1948. This was the year that the National Party government came to power in South Africa and started to put in place a number of laws to ensure white privilege by separating the 'races' through a policy that came to be known as apartheid. As a white person, I benefited from being born and growing up in a country and at a time when whites enjoyed all the trappings of power, and the attendant benefits of wealth and opportunity, which continued into my adult years.

My parents arrived in South Africa penniless, but back in Poland, as landowners, they had led a privileged existence. The significance of this was brought home to me when I came across my late parents' marriage certificate, which described my father as a 'landowner'. My father, who had obtained a degree in horticulture in France, had been farming on the family estate of Chmielowa for a few years when World War II broke out. When Germany invaded neighbouring Poland from the west on 1 September 1939, Chmielowa, deep in the southeast of the country and some ten kilometres from the Russian border, was a good distance away from the initial onslaught. So while the family was tense about the German aggression, they did not feel immediately threatened. In fact, they were able to give shelter in their barn and outbuildings to people fleeing from the west. But this sense of relative comfort was short-lived. During a Sunday lunch in mid-September, my father's uncle, who understood English, was listening to the BBC Overseas Service on the crackling valve radio. He heard that the Russian army had mobilised and was preparing to move into Poland. The area around Chmielowa was clearly endangered. Quick decisions had to be made.

While I was growing up, my father spoke little of these turbulent times. But in later years the family prevailed on him to write a mini-memoir. This succinct 25-page account, typed on his old Olivetti typewriter, begins with the pithy sentence, 'On 1st Sept. 1939 on the morning news on the radio we heard that Warsaw has been bombed by the German planes.' With considerable understatement he described their hasty departure from the family estate: 'with my wife who was soon expecting a baby, we packed quickly a few suitcases and within half an hour most of us were on the road.' What he did not say in this account, but what was to become part of family folklore, was that before they left, he and probably one or more of his three brothers buried the family silver somewhere in the forest between the homestead and the river below.

The idea of 'the family silver' may seem strange to modern readers. This is not a reference to items of great financial value. It means the table settings (cutlery, serving dishes, candlesticks and the like) that would be brought out to adorn the table on special occasions such as baptisms, weddings and religious feast days. Some might be family heirlooms, handed down from generation to generation, and often imprinted with the initials of the ancestor to whom they had been gifted. But at the time I did not ask my father what was in 'our' silver. I was only to find out much later.

I know that before they left the estate, my father and his brothers tried to persuade their father, my grandfather Adam, whose wife had died of Spanish flu many years earlier, to flee to Cracow. But he refused.

My heavily pregnant mother left Chmielowa in my uncle Kot's car, together with her suitcases, while my father accompanied them on his motorbike. They headed to the Dniester River where there was a ferry that would take them across to Romania. At that point, according to my father's memoir, 'my gardener Michał Jakowiec came and told me that some Jewish buyers wanted to buy some watermelons, but were offering a very low price. I told him to sell them for the best price he could, he manged to bring me some money before we boarded the ferry.'

Decades later my uncle Kot recounted how my mother had packed their old linen, thinking it would only be a 'little war' and that they would return to their comfortable manor house within a few months. But that never happened, as following the war Chmielowa became part of the USSR, while the four brothers ended up spread around the world: Ignacy in California, Andrzej in Cornwall in the UK, Kot (Konstantin) in France, and my father, Gustaw, in South Africa. Their father (my *Dziadzio*), who had refused to flee with his sons, remained behind the Iron Curtain. Sadly, neither my father nor any of his three brothers were ever to see him again, although he lived until 1960.

After crossing the Dniester the brothers split up. My parents made their way overland through Romania, where their first child, Adam, was born. In his memoir my father details how soon after arriving in Romania, he decided to lease a piece of land to farm and 'had to sell a golden snuff box which I had from Poland and which I was using as a cigarette case'. In October 1940, having just established the farm, he learned that the Romanian government, which had been very good to Polish refugees, had had to bow to German pressure and was about to force the refugees back to either Siberia or Polish concentration camps. He sought the advice of a Princess Ghica and her family, who evidently 'were helping many Polish refugees and took a great interest in my family'. Through her advice and good office – she arranged visas including transit visas through Turkey – my father decided to travel to Palestine with his young family. And then my father continues: 'I think it was 2 days later that we got our Passports back from the Princess, and she sent us her Rolls-Royce to fetch us from the farm to the railway station.' Unfortunately, I do not seem to have inherited my father's charm and panache to inveigle help from royalty.

Not long afterwards, Romania was invaded by the Soviets. By this time the family had moved on, crossing the Black Sea and landing in Istanbul. From here they travelled to Cairo, where *Tatuś* joined the Allied forces, under the command of the renowned Polish general Władysław Anders, while *Mama* worked for the Polish Red Cross.

It was during these war years that my three sisters were born – Wanda and Krysia in Haifa and Tel Aviv respectively (both cities were then in Palestine) and Marysia in Cairo. Sadly, my brother Adam had, in the meantime, died in Palestine. A haemophiliac like me, he had suffered an internal stomach bleed and succumbed before my parents could get him to hospital.

At the end of the war, when Churchill, Roosevelt and Stalin met at Yalta to redraw the boundaries of Eastern Europe, eastern Poland, including my father's home town, Lwów, and the family estate, Chmielowa, were excised from Poland and put under the yoke of the USSR. Given these circumstances, my parents were unable to return to their homeland. And so, a couple of years after the end of the war, they made a momentous decision. Together with their three young daughters, they travelled by ship through the Suez Canal and down the east coast of Africa, landing in Durban in 1948.

*

It is Christmas Eve 1958, and we are living on Cotswold farm, on the outskirts of Durbanville, to which we had moved from L'Ormarins. I am six years old and eyeing the freshly harvested pine tree, which I have helped my older sister Krysia decorate earlier that day. There is a star on top and many other decorations that I remember from previous years. We have carefully clipped some tiny candles, each with its own base, to the pine needles. I help to light the ones lower down. My father tells me to be careful not to burn the farmhouse down when I singe a pine needle, resulting in a crackling sound and a funny smell. There is a crib alongside, containing real straw that I have gathered from the cowshed to place in the crib and among the three kings, the shepherds and their sheep. Some glittering presents have mysteriously appeared under the tree and I wonder which one is for me. My father and two other sisters, Wanda and Marysia, appear. They look freshly scrubbed in their Sunday best.

My father, as in previous years, goes to each of my three sisters holding a paper-thin wafer that has been blessed by a priest; it has been sent to us by some unknown aunt in Poland. After congratulating Wanda on her excellent school results, he invites her to break off a piece of wafer, which she places on her tongue before he blesses each of us by making a cross on our foreheads. He does the same with the other two sisters, encouraging Krysia to work harder, then Marysia. Finally, it is my turn. He tells me that next year is going to be a big one as I will be starting school. Then comes my favourite part: the singing of Christmas carols, such as 'Hosanna in the highest' and 'Silent night', in Polish on our farm in Africa. When it is time for me to select a carol, I choose one about the birds and animals coming to pay homage at the crib. It's my best, as I love imitating the different sounds the creatures make.

But I sense that something is wrong, very wrong. *Mama* is lying on a sickbed in an adjoining, darkened bedroom, which I am not allowed to enter in case I disturb her. Nobody has told me what is wrong with her. But I remember the day Count Ludek Cieński came from Franschhoek to visit *Tatuś*. I had crept under the coffee table, listening to their conversation. *Tatuś* described taking *Mama* to hospital, from where she'd returned just a few days earlier. 'It was too late,' I heard my father say in Polish. 'They opened her up and there was just *rak*.' Although I am unaware that the word means 'cancer', I can feel that something tragic is looming.

But now we are singing carols heartily in Polish – our first language.

*

It is my first day at school, in Kenridge, a suburb of Durbanville. Mama makes the huge effort of getting up from her sickbed to accompany my father to see me start my school career. She feebly waves goodbye from the passenger seat of the car as I make my way in trepidation down the school driveway to join the file of children lining up. I am told by a large, friendly-looking lady to hold the hand of the boy next to me, which I nervously do.

I was then seven years old, Later that year I was taken to spend some time with *Ciocia* Jadzia Miszewska and her family in Pinelands. This Cape Town suburb, known as the 'garden city', was very different from the dustbowl farm of my childhood years. The Miszewski family had four sons, and Kuba was my playmate.

I recollect, some sixty years later, that *Ciocia* Jadzia told us two boys to go and wait outside in the driveway: 'We are going to walk to the shops and I will be there in a minute.' As I sat basking in the autumnal sun, the earth seemed to move: a kind of rocking, dipping feeling, and then it stabilised. It felt strange, but I thought little more of it at the time.

Later that afternoon, the elderly Todeschini couple, Italian friends of our family, came to pick me up in their maroon-and-fawn van to take me home to Cotswold. On the way, Mrs Todeschini asked me why I looked so sad. I must have intuited the worst. I somehow sensed that something terrible had happened.

As I entered the front door of our rambling old house, my father greeted me and walked alongside me, his hand on my shoulder. '*Mama umarła*,' he said. Mother has died. He led me to the familiar room where she had spent many cancer-racked days and months, sometimes screaming in agony – sounds I blotted from my mind, but which one of my sisters later reminded me of.

She looked calm and at peace and more beautiful than I had ever seen her. I did not cry. Sometime later, I overheard much discussion among the Polish *ciotki* (aunts) and others as to whether I should attend her funeral. In the end I did, but I have no recollection of the Mass that would have been held. I remember throwing some red soil as her coffin was lowered. I did not cry then, either. Instead, as I was to realise years later, I put a concrete band around my seven-year-old heart, so as not to allow anyone in who could cause me such pain again. Her death was also the cause of years of intermittent depression.

A second long-term consequence for me of my mother's premature death was an inexplicable longing for Poland, although I had never been there and it was virtually inaccessible behind the Iron Curtain. Perhaps this longing was absorbed from my mother, who never felt at home in South Africa.

I was later to find out that my mother had died at about ten o'clock in the morning, while I was waiting for *Ciocia* Jadzia to go shopping, and when I had felt that strange, disorientating sensation. Her death affected me deeply, but not in a way I could understand at the time. As a teenager, whenever my sister Krysia referred to our mother, I could not say the word *Mama* nor respond with any enthusiasm to the framed picture of her she held out to me.

*

In the months after my mother died, a frequent visitor to Cotswold was my godmother, *Ciocia* Tychna. She would often make the long trip from the Elgin apple farm managed by Stefan Komornicki, where she lived, to visit my father on Sundays. She wore checked woollen skirts and fawn tops and smelled of fragrant soap, like a princess, I thought. And indeed, she *was* a princess, albeit a chubby, warm and cuddly one, her full title being Princess Tychna Puzyna, having married Prince Stefan Puzyna, who had died years before.

She always had something for me in her big, cluttered handbag. 'Guess what I have in here for you here today?' she would typically ask. I would eagerly rummage through all the paraphernalia – lipsticks, hairclips, buttons and other mysterious objects – until I came across the sought-after treasure: a roll of humbugs or colourful sweets with a hole in them that I would suck for ages. And she always brought a carton of vanilla Wall's Ice Cream for pudding. Once she bathed me, making me stand up in the bath and rubbing white soap all over my scrawny body. 'Now you are a tennis player – ready for Wimbledon!' she announced in Polish. Delighted, I plunged back into the warm water.

Ciocia Tychna always wore long sleeves, even on the hottest of Cape summer days. This was to hide the numbers tattooed above her wrist while she was in Auschwitz. She never talked about it. Years later, I was to learn that as a PhD graduate from what was then Jan Kazimierz University in Lwów, she worked for the Polish underground in Cracow, where the Nazis set up their headquarters. She spied for the Polish underground while waitressing in a high-class restaurant frequented by German officers. But she was betrayed by one of her colleagues and was sent to Auschwitz.

Here she was assigned to work in a quarry, breaking and carrying rocks. She developed typhoid, and it was while in the hospital that she was pointed out to Josef Mengele, the notorious physician at the camp, as the former star PhD graduate in anthropology of her Polish professor. A few years before the war, Mengele had visited the Polish professor who was supervising Tychna's PhD studies in Lwów. He was introduced to this attractive young doctoral student, who had shown him around. They now met again under very different circumstances in the death camp. Mengele hauled her out of the hospital, arranged superior treatment for her, and suggested that she rather work for him. That probably saved her life.

After the war she never talked of her experiences in Auschwitz. She was aware of the value of research, but at the same time she was tormented by her role as assistant to Mengele. That is probably why she remained silent and never resumed her research work after the war. Some of this story is recorded in the book on Mengele by Gerald Posner and John Ward, who interviewed her in her latter years in London.

Ciocia Tychna was a firm favourite of the children in the close-knit Polish community in the Cape during my growing-up years. We all loved her and to this day speak fondly of her.

In the 1970s, *Ciocia* Tychna decided to leave South Africa to settle in London. I was a student at the time and recall rushing from Kenilworth racecourse, where I worked on Saturdays on the tote, to Cape Town harbour. She was leaving on the *Pendennis Castle*, and the entire local Polish community had gathered on the dock, including my father and stepmother. On seeing me, my stepmother chided, 'You look like a bedraggled orphan off the street, look at you – dirty, torn trousers, unkempt long hair.' What image was I trying to project?

Many years later, during my first trip to Europe at the age of 21, I went to visit *Ciocia* Tychna in her Ealing home in London. She suggested we go shopping. We set off down the high street. I felt slightly uncomfortable yet pleased when she hooked her arm through mine as we walked past all the shiny shops. Steering me into Marks & Spencer, she directed me to the men's section. She bought me a thick cream-coloured polo-neck jersey to fend off the London cold. About twenty years later, after it had kept me warm through many winters, I reluctantly gave the jersey to a beggar who knocked on my door. I hope it kept him warm too.

After she died, I asked my friend Jadzia about her last days. She recounted how *Ciocia* Tychna was confused and drifted in and out of consciousness in her Polish nursing home in Ealing, where Jadzia visited her. When she was leaving, she asked Jadzia how she was getting home. 'The underground, as usual,' Jadzia replied. 'Be careful of the Nazis in the tunnels,' she warned. That is the only time I know of that she referred – indirectly – to her time in Auschwitz.

My childhood dream of *Tatuś* marrying *Ciocia* Tychna was shattered when I became a weekly boarder with the Edwards family on the edge of the village of Durbanville, so as to be close to school. That is when my father got to know widowed Mrs Edwards better.

CHAPTER 2

A Farm Called Cotswold

IT WAS at Cotswold that I spent most of the first seven years of my life. The Cotswolds in England have been declared an 'area of outstanding natural beauty', mainly because of the rolling green hills, quaint villages and stately homes. In contrast, 'our' Cotswold was stony, windswept, dry and dusty. *Tatuś* complained more than once that all the land was good for was its stones and, indeed, today it is a quarry.

The farmhouse, set far back from the public road, was flanked by a massive out-of-place palm tree, where I used to play in the dust. Its mud-brick walls were whitewashed and its sloping corrugated-iron roof was painted red. Cotswold was seven miles from Durbanville. To get to the village, one left the house along a narrow, bluegum-lined driveway that led onto the public gravel road. One then wound one's way past rocky outcrops and alongside the rolling wheatfields of a succession of farms belonging to the Starke, Van der Westhuizen and Louw families. An adjoining farm was owned by one Botha, whom my father referred to derisively as a real 'boer', presumably after some disagreement. Eventually, one reached the village on a tarred road.

On one of the few occasions that my mother drove the old Standard Vanguard to the village, I recollect her terror when she wanted to overtake the slow-moving farm trucks that trundled along the road. 'Go, go, go...' I remember saying silently to myself. She would also pick up the farm labourers' kids who were walking home from school, and when they thanked her she struggled to say in Afrikaans 'Maak nie saak nie' (no problem), despite practising the phrase.

My mother often talked about Poland, and spoke with great fondness of her sister, *Ciocia* Wanda, showing me photographs of her children, Paweł and Magda. My first cousin Paweł was to accompany me on my first trip to Chmielowa many decades later.

My father, in contrast, spoke little about his pre-war years. But I did get an occasional glimpse of his life then, for example, when he mentioned that as youngsters he and his three brothers had a French governess. Recently, I came across some research on my father's brother, *Strij* Andrzej – a mystical priest – by Paul Kieniewicz, who knew my uncle from his teenage years. A letter written by Andrzej to a friend gave me some insight not only into my uncle but also the lifestyle of my father and my grandparents:

> I [Andrzej] was born 2 March 1905 in south-eastern Poland, and at the time under the Austrian regime, of rich cultural parents. My father was a judge, and as a young man became a kind of Lord Lieutenant in the county, having also a large property of land. A man of highest integrity, he became later a politician of renown in Poland, leading a national party, and an association of aristocracy in south-eastern Poland...
>
> In such a milieu I was brought up, in the best possible schools – studies at the university, first law, then anthropology, the history of art, and also studied music in a conservatory, leading a gay life and sporty one too. Hunting, shooting, fencing, tennis, swimming, ice skating, skiing. Very fond of dancing and girls. *Un bon viveur* – sort of.

I also learned about my father's other brothers, who had left Poland as young men at the outbreak of World War II. But it was *Strij* Andrzej who intrigued me most. He started studying law at Jan Kazimierz University in Lwów but gave that up to study theology in Rome. After he was ordained as a Catholic priest, he first served in Rohatyn, a town now in Ukraine. I drove through Rohatyn on my various visits to Chmielowa, noticing a striking Rococo stone church, but not realising that this was where he probably ministered to the locals. When war broke out, *Strij* Andrzej left Chmielowa, ending up in Rome for a while before settling in England, where he served in a parish in Cornwall. He was not a conventional priest and was reputed to have psychic and healing powers. I was told that he was able to see 'auras' and could also diagnose illness upon first meeting the afflicted person. Apart from working with people's 'energy fields', he dabbled in the field of radiotronics and wrote academic papers on the subject. He would write to my mother, advising her how to use her hands and healing energy to treat my internal bleeds as a child – techniques she applied to my swollen knees and ankles, though without apparent success. My father merely shook his head and chuckled whenever Andrzej's mystical powers came up in conversation.

I never met *Strij* Andrzej, but his name often popped up in unexpected places. Once I came across a small book titled *Healing through Colour*, whose author stated in the preface: 'Thus I see that Rudolf Steiner brings the spiritual thinking, Pierre Teilhard de Chardin adds the spiritual action of will, and my friend Andrew Glazewski the universal love; while Carl Jung opens the soul of man and looks deeply into the images which feature in the visions of each individual.' Similarly, the preface to a book that Paul Kieniewicz wrote on Andrzej says: 'Forty years after his death, people talk about him as an extraordinary person who changed their lives.'

Apart from Polish, my father was fluent in French and German, and had a rudimentary knowledge of Russian, Romanian and later

Afrikaans. He also studied English while travelling by boat with his young family down the East African coast, before disembarking in Durban. He had little in common with the local neighbours. Instead, he connected with other former rural landowners who had also left the region of Galicia in eastern Poland at the outbreak of the war. They formed the nucleus of his network in South Africa. A handful of them had come to South Africa in the belief that the agricultural and other prospects in this country were promising. It was my father's friend Franek Rozwadowski who led the way, having emigrated to South Africa very soon after World War II. He came from the same region in Poland and formed a 'chain of friendship', encouraging my father and other Poles to join him as farmers in the Western Cape.

Franek Rozwadowski worked as the manager of Applethwaite farm in Grabouw, before moving to Somerset West, where he managed Lourensford. Stefan Komornicki then took over the management of Applethwaite. Two other Poles, George Rosenwerth and Bolesław Herbowicz, managed various functions on Applethwaite, including the orchards and infrastructure, as well as the workshop and cold storage plant. The office on the farm was run by my beloved godmother, *Ciocia* Tychna Puzyna. It was this group of Poles who laid the groundwork for the huge success of apple farming operations in the district, which led not only to the development of a vibrant international export market for fresh fruit, but also to Appletiser fruit juice, which today enjoys an international reputation.

Other families prominent in my childhood included the Miszewskis, whose son Kuba I used to play with, and the Rosenwerths – Elżbieta Rosenwerth became a leading haute couture designer, one of South Africa's first. Our family's social activities in those early days centred around these and other members of the growing Polish community, all of whom arrived in the Cape after the war. On special occasions, our families would typically congregate for a picnic lunch and drinks at a farm dam, where we kids would swim and enjoy ourselves.

Though short and slightly built, cheerful *Ciocia* Ala Komornicka – who was not an actual relative – exuded energy. She initiated the annual gathering of Cape Town's Polish clan on Boxing Day (St Stephen's Day), which was also the name day of her husband, Stefan. These lunchtime get-togethers – where we partook of cold sliced beef and fresh garden salads, and ended with strawberries and vanilla ice cream, all accompanied by much vodka – went on until well after midnight. *Ciocia* Ala would invariably be found dancing Cossack-style, encircled by other rowdy, somewhat inebriated Poles. She was the life and soul of these parties.

When my mother was dying, *Ciocia* Ala rushed to her bedside with a bunch of blue irises that she had nicked from her neighbour's dining-room table in Grabouw. Decades later, she and her husband moved to Ealing in London, and 15 Carlton Road became a home from home for me whenever I visited the city. Years later, I travelled to London for her memorial service, and paid tribute to her on behalf of the South African Polish clan. It was important for me to connect with my childhood roots and with the Polish diaspora I had grown up with, many of whom had in the meantime returned to Europe.

The Rozwadowskis, Komornickis, Miszewskis, Rosenwerths, Herbowiczes, Jurystowskis and their children formed my world, even though we only saw them on special occasions, isolated as we were on Cotswold farm. This post-war wave of Poles was very different from the second wave of Polish immigrants who came out in the late 1980s and early 1990s, during the time of the Solidarity movement and the state of emergency in Poland. Some of them had engineering or technical skills and were actively recruited and welcomed by the apartheid government.

During the Easter weekend of 1993, I was with a group of friends enjoying a holiday and celebrating a colleague's birthday in Bulawayo, Zimbabwe, when we heard the news that Chris Hani, the general secretary of the South African Communist Party, and a champion of the liberation movement, had been assassinated. Our celebrations were brought to a sharp halt as we contemplated the implications for South Africa, then sitting on a knife edge. I vividly recollect Nelson Mandela, who was not yet president, making an impassioned plea on television for calm, as the country could easily have exploded into bloody revolution. I felt a sense of shame that the assassin was a Pole. Janusz Waluś had emigrated from Poland to avoid the oppressive communist regime, but murdering Hani, allegedly in the name of 'anti-communism', was a tragic, thoughtless act. Months later, the town council of Waluś's home town in Poland proposed naming a street after the killer, to my outrage. Fortunately, that did not happen, as the Polish government realised it would cause a major diplomatic furore with the future democratic government in South Africa, which was then on the threshold of power.

Years previously, while I was doing my articles with a Johannesburg law firm, I had defended a coloured builder from the Cape who had contravened the Group Areas Act by living in Hillbrow (a 'white' area) with his girlfriend. At the same time, I met a Polish immigrant, a client at our law office, who had been given various incentives to come to South Africa, including a soft housing loan. While I was happy to meet a fellow Pole, the fact that he was being treated in this generous way by the apartheid government, in sharp contrast to my coloured client, made me feel very uncomfortable.

*

It was during my childhood on Cotswold that I recollect feeling pangs of loneliness, a feeling that has remained with me for much of my adult life. My mother was sick in bed, my father was out somewhere on the farm, and my sisters were at boarding school. I used to hang out with Frank, an Angolan who was the general factotum around the house.

Typically, I would walk about on the dusty farm, pulling a toy trailer behind me, looking for my friends Sydney, Korrie and Dawie, the labourers' kids. Much of my early childhood was spent mucking about with them. Their father drove the old farm tractor and let me sit on the seat with him. I learned Afrikaans from them, or, more accurately, Cape coloured Afrikaans, known as Kaaps, and it became my second language. Although I could read English, I only started speaking it at school.

We spent hours wandering around the farm exploring and amusing ourselves. I learned that if I peed on the same spot that Sydney did, it would make the large plantar wart on my hand disappear. Whenever I visited their home on the far side of the farm, their mother, Laine, fed us thick, piping-hot slices of white bread spread with homemade apricot jam.

As I grew up, I lost contact with my early childhood friends, as we did not attend the same schools in those apartheid days. I missed them.

*

At some stage during my mother's illness, my middle sister, Krysia, left Springfield Convent in Wynberg, where she was boarding, and came home to attend day school at Durbanville High, partly to be with our mother and partly to look after me. Krysia, who is eleven years older than me, became an anchor not only in my childhood but through to my adulthood. She was always there for me when I needed a meal, or a visitor in hospital, or felt at a loss on an empty Sunday. When she was on a gap year living in Vancouver during my teenage years, I missed her terribly. She was vibrant, popular and active. I recollect my father describing her in Polish as *sprytna*, meaning mercurial or sharp. During my early adult years I admonished her for nagging me about something. Her response was: 'The last words *Mama* said to me were "Look after Janek".' And she did just that, sometimes at the expense of her own children.

As I have said, I was not aware of what was wrong with *Mama*, who seemed always to be in her darkened room in a sickbed. *Ciocia* Tychna from the Elgin farm insisted we employ Sophie, a young woman, who would also help care for *Mama* and me. My favourite time of the day was bedtime, when Sophie would lie next to me and read exciting Enid Blyton books such as the Famous Five adventure series. While I lay curled up against Sophie, I would follow the words on the page, and I gradually started to read them myself. She would invariably snap the book shut at the end of the chapter, hug me, and go off to her room. But I was so excited by the machinations and escapades of George and her companions that I would then reopen the book and continue reading by myself. The next evening, Sophie would ask where we'd got to and then continue from where she'd left off. I dared not tell her that I had already surreptitiously read these chapters.

By the time I started school, I was reading entire Famous Five books and was somewhat perplexed when we started learning to read, and only two words, 'Old Lob', appeared on the first page, accompanied by a picture of an overweight farmer in striped overalls. Subsequent pages included drawings with accompanying words such as 'cow', 'pig', and so on. I was bored, as by then I was immersed in the sleuthing escapades of the Hardy Boys. I imagined myself as a detective and followed Tom and Dick's example by making observations about everything around me. Ever since, I have been an avid reader.

*

My mother died in October during my first year at school. Afterwards, all I seemingly had was my father and my sister Krysia. Once Krysia was old enough to drive, she or my father would take me to school at Kenridge Primary, where I spent the first two years of my schooling. I was sent to this small establishment on the outskirts of the village because my father did not want me to go to Durbanville Primary, a much bigger dual-medium school in the village. Who knew what might happen to a haemophiliac on its dusty playground at break?

It was at Kenridge Primary that I felt for the first time the very real and lifelong consequences of being a haemophiliac. At break we all rushed to the playground to play cricket. But immediately I was told by one of the teachers to hold back and stay on the sidelines – this would remain my lot throughout my school years. I was seven years old at the time, and my best friend in Grade 2 was Garth, a well-built, stocky boy who looked as if he would make a good rugby forward one day. After being invited to his home one Saturday, I accompanied him to watch his father play cricket for the local club. While the men were out on the field, I lobbed a cricket ball to Garth, the 'opening batsman', who blocked it a few times, and then whacked it straight at me, hitting me in the left eye. By the time the men came for their lunch break, I had a huge black-and-blue eye and had to be taken home immediately and then on to the hospital for a transfusion of the blood-clotting factor. I don't recollect any more outings to Garth – or to any other boys – after that.

There were only seven or eight pupils in our Grade 1 class, so we shared a classroom with the Grade 2 and Grade 3 children. Mrs Mashford, a plump lady whom I liked very much, taught us all simultaneously. At the end of my first school year, I brought my report card home. It was lunchtime on a hot day, and the southeaster was blowing up eucalyptus-scented dust as usual outside our house. I took the report card from my satchel and handed it in trepidation to my father, who was seated at the head of the dark, oval dining-room table. His portrait, commissioned sometime during World War II, hung ominously above him. He read: 'Reading – A; Afrikaans – A; Geography – A; Arithmetic – A; Spelling – A.' And then he repeated; 'Writing – C. Writing – C!', crying out: 'You'd better improve your writing!'

I was devastated. I was born left-handed, but when my father first noticed me trying to write my name, he said this was not to be. He duly instructed Mrs Mashford: 'This boy is to write right-handed!' Many years later, when I questioned him about this, he said that this was how it was in pre-war Poland. You were disadvantaged if you were left-handed: surgical implements, for example, were designed for right-handed people, and so were scissors. I was not to be *sinestra*.

As an adult I would be somewhat consoled when I read that the proportion of left-handed people in the population who are creative or high achievers far outweighs their right-handed counterparts. Many artists are left-handed, and the proportion of left-handed American presidents (including Barack Obama) is far greater than the national average of left-handed people. During my twenties I came across a book titled *Drawing on the Right Side of the Brain* and I couldn't help wondering what effect writing with the 'wrong side' of my brain might have had on me.

*

After my mother died, *Tatuś* continued to eke out a living on Cotswold farm. Among his problems was the daily trip to take me to Kenridge Primary School. Although the daily trip was time-consuming and expensive, he did not want to risk my being injured while hopping on and off the farm school bus, which trundled past our farm on its way to the much larger and predominantly Afrikaans Durbanville Primary School. I had no idea that the eventual solution to this problem would be found unexpectedly during our attendance at Sunday morning Mass at the Catholic church in the village.

CHAPTER 3

Vygeboom Days

'I'M GOING to marry Mrs Edwards,' my father announced matter-of-factly one day in late 1961, a year or so after the death of my mother. My heart sank. I had been hoping he would marry my godmother, *Ciocia* Tychna.

We were well acquainted with the Edwards family. Like us, their clan of eight children – four boys and four girls – religiously attended Sunday morning Mass at the local Catholic church, which was tucked away in a cul-de-sac in the centre of Durbanville. The Edwardses often arrived a little late, in their clapped-out, dusty Rolls-Royce. A seemingly endless number of kids would tumble out, not only from the back doors but also from an open boot. Their flamboyant father, Launce Edwards, a land surveyor with an eye for land with development potential, had bought Vygeboom, which adjoined a suburb in the village. He suffered a heart attack at the age of 49, leaving behind his wife, Kathleen, and their eight children. The oldest, Peter, was 18, while the youngest, Marcelle, was a baby of 18 months.

After Sunday morning Mass, the adults would troop out and enjoy cheese sandwiches and tea. On one such occasion Mrs Edwards asked my recently widowed father, 'How are things going?'

'I'm struggling to travel twice daily to take Janek to school and back,' he replied. My father then told Mrs Edwards that he was thinking of sending me as a weekly boarder to Nazareth House, an orphanage in Vredehoek, on the slopes of Table Mountain just above the Cape Town city centre. It seemed a hundred miles away at the time.

'Oh nonsense!' I overheard her reply. 'He must come stay with us. I have to cart my children to school every day, and one more will not make a difference.'

Thus it was that, soon afterwards, I found myself thrust into this large, bewildering family of eight as a weekly boarder. I was very unhappy boarding with the Edwards family. I just wanted to be with *Tatuś*, who was battling away on Cotswold. I missed him terribly, only seeing him at weekends. I recollect once, on his birthday, 12 September, I must have been looking extremely dejected because Mrs Edwards asked me what was wrong. I said it was my father's birthday and I wanted to buy him a present. She gave me a sixpence, and I bought him some sweets at Mr Pantelli's local café. I actually wanted to buy him some gloves, as he'd mentioned that his skin was dry, but they cost too much.

Because Mrs Edwards's farm abutted the village of Durbanville, it was no problem for her to drop me off at Kenridge School, which was close to the school her sons John and Martin attended. She, being widowed, was having difficulty managing Vygeboom, which was more of a going concern than Cotswold. It was not so much a farm as an expansive smallholding, which included a large dam established by her late husband.

At weekends, my father would pick me up from Kathleen's rambling old double-storey farmhouse. The two of them got to know each during these weekly rendezvous, and their relationship was sealed when my father invited her to Cotswold for Krysia's 19th birthday celebration.

My father's announcement that he was going to marry Mrs Edwards shattered me. I have no recollection of their wedding day. The only reminder of that day is a photograph that graced the mantelpiece in the lounge of the rambling Vygeboom home until my stepmother's death decades later. It was taken at the reception and shows my father looking dapper in his tailor-made summer suit beside Aunt Kathleen beaming like a newlywed, together with what was at the time their menagerie of twelve children: my three sisters and me; the four Edwards girls, including the twins and baby Marcelle in Janet's arms; and the four Edwards boys: Peter, Paul, and then John and Martin, who were close in age to me. The merger of the two families was sufficiently newsworthy to warrant a report in *Die Burger*, the Afrikaans daily newspaper.

Kathleen came from colonial stock: her father, Brigadier Morris, served in the British colonial government in India before being transferred to Rhodesia, where he became head of the BSAP (British South Africa Police). I remember his presence while I was a boarder with the Edwardses, but he eventually left for Rhodesia, where he died soon after. His ceremonial sword was kept in my stepbrother John's upstairs room and was often brandished by John and Martin. Morris Depot – named after the Brigadier – is police headquarters in Harare to this day. (Later, in my years as a lecturer at university, mentioning to my Zimbabwean students that I was indirectly related to the late Brigadier invariably brought squawks of delight and admiration, to my surprise.)

When my father and Kathleen married, the two eldest children of the combined family were already students: Wanda was at Stellenbosch University, while Peter had begun medical studies at the University of Cape Town (UCT). I vividly recall feeling bereft as my father and his bride drove off to honeymoon at the Lanzerac Hotel in Stellenbosch, leaving us boys and Marcelle in the care of my new older sister, Janet. In the months after their return, my father relocated from the dustbowl of Cotswold to the lush pastures of Vygeboom, which bordered the adjoining and expanding suburb of Valmary Park.

The newlyweds, both devout Catholics, added two more children to the menagerie: Andrzej (Andrew), named after our mystical uncle, and Adela, named after my paternal grandmother who had succumbed to the Spanish flu. From an age point of view, I fell right in the middle of the siblings. As a 13-year-old, I would often push Adela around in a pram under the huge leafy trees in the garden at Vygeboom.

After moving to Vygeboom, my father developed a large vegetable patch below the dam, which we called the 'bottom ground'. Together, my father and his new wife set up a farm stall on Durbanville Avenue, bordering the farm; it was the main artery from Durbanville to the highway leading to Cape Town. We sold not only a variety of fresh vegetables harvested from the bottom ground but also table chickens, fresh milk, cream and butter – all from the farm. My father would get up at sunrise, drive down to the bottom ground, and, together with two or three Xhosa labourers, pick vegetables for the day, which he delivered to the farm stall. His timing was perfectly set so that he would be back at his bedroom washbasin at eight o'clock sharp, to shave while listening to the morning news. He would then go for a hearty breakfast prepared by Aunt Kathleen. During the school holidays, I whiled away the hours at the farm stall, helping Wilson, a Xhosa man who wore thick-rimmed spectacles without lenses, to sell our produce.

In addition to his vegetable patch, my father developed a large strawberry field on the farm. At one point, Sunday lunch comprised a home-grown feast of roast chicken, potatoes and vegetables, followed by fresh strawberries and cream. The hand-picked strawberries we ate were those that could not be sold as they had been pecked by the birds. But, in fact, they were the most delicious. The strawberries ripened in the heat of summer, and on Sundays there was no labour to harvest the fruit. So, Aunt Kathleen phoned Father O'Brien, the local Catholic priest, to seek permission for us kids to work on a Sunday. The picking had to be done at dawn on the hot summer days, before the birds swooped in to ruin the brightest of the fast-ripening strawberries. The long rows of strawberries seemed endless, the work was back-breaking, and I am no longer a great fan of strawberries.

Among the Xhosa labourers on Vygeboom was Douglas, who came with us from Cotswold, and who milked the cows. The Edwardses' domestic worker was Matilda. She would invariably ask when I walked into the kitchen, 'Ufuna ntoni?' (What are you looking for?). From her I learned this and other Xhosa words, such as *ndilambile* (I'm hungry).

I had already become aware of apartheid, for, on the last day of every month, the three or four black staff members would troop into my father's office at Cotswold and have their pass books signed. Scorned as the *dompas* (stupid pass), this was one of apartheid's ways of controlling the movement of black people. It was on Vygeboom farm where I caught my first real glimpse of the cruelty of the apartheid system, when an unannounced police raid occurred right in front of our house. I recollect dignified, middle-aged Matilda stumbling while running to hide behind the loquat trees, as the police searched for offenders who were not carrying a pass book.

I cannot remember exactly when, but it was during my early teenage years that I stopped calling my stepmother 'Aunt Kathleen' and simply used 'Mom'.

*

My eldest stepbrother, Peter, was in his final year of school when his father died. He woke up that morning to learn that he would now be the man of the family, which has burdened him throughout the rest of his life. After Peter came Janet, some ten years older than me. Years later, Janet recounted that sometime after my mother was diagnosed with cancer, she arrived unannounced at Vygeboom. This was rather uncharacteristic as, although the two families knew each other from church, they did not socialise. *Mama* asked if she could look around the spacious double-storey farmhouse with its white-painted walls and distinctive silver-grey zinc roof. She must have intuited the future, for on leaving after twenty minutes or so she indicated that she approved of the homestead. It seems that she had my father's well-being and mine in mind.

The Vygeboom farmhouse was altered to accommodate the four Glazewski children. Upstairs was a large dusty loft, which was converted into three bedrooms and a large playroom. Later, this space encouraged us teenagers to stay at home on weekend nights rather than roam the streets of Durbanville. It was as if my mother had envisaged this kind of safe space when she approved the homestead shortly before her death.

Together with John, who was a year older than me, and Martin, a year younger, we were always referred to as 'the three boys'. 'The three boys must have a bath', 'The three boys must have a haircut', and so on. During these teenage years, my eldest stepbrother, Peter, who was studying medicine, would take the three of us to explore the outdoors. I vividly recollect climbing Skeleton Gorge on Table Mountain in great excitement, camping on the mountain, and lighting a campfire, which was then allowed. He introduced us to bird-watching, which I enjoy to this day. I was jealous of Martin, who had excellent eyesight and could spot and identify a bird a mile away.

In those teenage and early adult years, Peter was someone I looked up to. When John and I were in Grade 10, Peter invited us three boys to Oshakati in what was then northern South West Africa, where he was doing his housemanship. The three-day train journey was itself an adventure. We explored the remote region, sleeping in the open veld, next to a fire, while lions roared nearby. We arrived at the Cunene River on a typically hot day; here I recollect swimming and only hearing about the possibility of crocodiles afterwards. I utterly loved being in the bush and gaining first-hand knowledge of the fascinating Himba people.

South Africa was still unlawfully occupying the territory, having refused to surrender the League of Nations mandate that it had been given to govern the territory after World War I. At the time of our visit, nearby Ondangwa was the headquarters of the South African Air Force, which was involved in the drawn-out Border War with Angola. The heavy presence of South African military personnel was in sharp contrast to the wide open spaces, and put a damper on our adventure in what was still one of the wild parts of southern Africa. I could not have known at the time that my eventual career as an environmental lawyer would be shaped by Namibia's independence in 1990.

Although he was a year younger than me, Martin was physically much stronger. He seemed to have two distinct sides. One was a gentle, generous soul who would give his last shirt away on a rainy day to a poor passer-by; then, seemingly for no reason, he would snap into a wholly other aggressive persona. I have a vivid recollection of him pelting me with acorns underneath the old oak tree in front of the family home, and cowering while he assailed me, laughing hysterically all the while. The sting and hurt I can feel to this day. In retrospect, I guess I should be grateful. It was an important, formative character-building period of my life, as I had entered the Edwards family from a background where my three older sisters treated their haemophiliac brother like a vulnerable little boy who needed looking after. Martin, along with the older John, taught me to fend for myself in a hostile world. My father, who was too preoccupied with keeping the Edwards–Glazewski family constellation together, was not there to protect me.

*

After I completed Grades 1 and 2 at Kenridge, it was decided that we three boys should together attend St Vincent de Paul, a Catholic convent in Bellville. We caught the bus daily on the then majestic Durbanville Avenue, which bordered the farm, with its characteristic avenue of bluegums. The bus fare was one cent, and when the fare went up to one and a half cents, my father exclaimed, 'That's a fifty per cent increase!'

After alighting in Voortrekker Road, we walked for ten minutes to our new school. The nuns said that when we passed the Catholic church en route, we had to make the sign of the cross to purge us of venal sins. If we committed too many venal sins, our souls would become completely black, and if we died in this state we'd go straight to hell. The solution, they told us, was to go to confession and do penance afterwards. But if we committed a mortal sin, there was no chance of redemption and we would be eternally damned.

After two years at St Vincent de Paul, the three of us changed schools again, to attend Durbanville Primary School, one mile's walk from Vygeboom. We were joined by my youngest stepsister, Marcelle, who was then just starting school. As we used to walk through the suburb of Valmary Park, a stern-looking Senator Van Nierop would shout at us boys from his balcony to carry Marcelle's school bag for her. We developed the strategy that one of us would take Marcelle's bag from her as we approached Van Nierop's house and hand it back to her as soon as we passed by.

Durbanville Primary was officially a dual-medium school, although it was predominantly Afrikaans. Apart from the standard subjects such as arithmetic and English grammar, religious instruction (RI) was taught once a week. This was tailored to the strict Calvinist tradition observed by most Afrikaners at the time. At the start of the period the teacher would announce, 'Catholics and Jews, out!' So I would have to troop out, along with a handful of Jewish classmates, and sit on the floor in the cold corridor. This suited me perfectly, as I used to sit next to my best friend, Colin Scher, and compare notes about the Top 20 on the LM Radio hit parade, broadcast the previous Sunday evening.

After two years at Durbanville Primary, we three boys were enrolled as weekly boarders at St Joseph's Marist College in Rondebosch to continue our Catholic education. I was in Grade 7 and was immediately drawn to my class teacher, Mr Kenny, a lay teacher among the many

Irish brothers, who was also the first team rugby coach. I recall feeling embarrassed when, on my first or second day at our new school, Mr Kenny sat next to me at my desk in front of the whole class to help me with my wretched, now right-handed, handwriting. Still, he was a wonderful teacher. I'd arrive home on a Friday afternoon and eagerly recount to my father, who was seated at his roll-top desk, the fascinating things Mr Kenny had taught us in the science class that week. Invariably, my stepmother would walk in and exclaim, 'Hm, what are you two talking about?' I sensed that, for some inexplicable reason, she did not approve of my close relationship with my father.

Often, though, instead of going home for the weekend, I would remain at school on a Friday night so that I could watch the first team play the next morning. For 'away' games, I would get a lift with Mr Kenny along with one or two players in the team. This, to some extent, made up for my inability to participate in sporting activities. Not only was I a rugby linesman for a short while, but Mr Kenny also made me the first-team cricket scorer, and later in Grade 8 he recruited me to run the tuckshop. When the sweaty boys trooped off the playing field, they would come to me to buy their Coke and sweets. At the time, I had a recurrent series of internal bleeds into my left knee and Mr Kenny took me to Groote Schuur Hospital to have my factor VIII infusion. His kindness both pleased and bewildered me as a young boy.

Around this time, my middle sister, Krysia, went abroad, taking a gap year. I missed her and used to talk a lot about her to Mr Kenny. On her return to South Africa, she once dropped us three boys at the boarding school, as was the custom on a Sunday evening, and met Mr Kenny. He ended up asking her out and marrying her soon after. By then I was in Grade 10.

*

I performed well academically at St Joseph's, no doubt because I tried harder in the classroom as I could not perform on the sports field. I was in the A-stream class, which included Latin as a subject (this proved useful at university, as it was a compulsory subject at the time for law students). My elder stepbrother, John, failed a year, so we ended up in the same class, although in different streams. Martin, who was a grade below me, was also struggling academically. Towards the end of Grade 10, our parents called us for a special meeting under the large oak tree at Vygeboom and announced that they were thinking of sending us three boys to Wynberg Boys' High, where John and Martin could do woodwork and metalwork, subjects that were not offered at St Joseph's.

Mom, standing alongside my father, asked me, 'How do you feel about this, Jan?'

I felt very uncomfortable, as I was happy at St Joseph's College. But I did not want to rock the family boat: having us three boys in different schools would inconvenience my parents. So, I reluctantly agreed. Thus it was that I found myself in my fifth and, thankfully, final school for Grades 11 and 12 at Wynberg Boys' High School, along with John and Martin. Martin attended the boarding school, but my parents decided that John and I would be weekly boarders at the home of my newly wed sister Krysia and her husband, Kevin, formerly Mr Kenny, at the latter's suggestion. He had left St Joseph's just before he married my sister. They had bought a small house near the Newlands stadium, and John and I commuted daily by train to our new school. While I had felt very comfortable and happy at my former school, I found Wynberg large and bewildering and never felt at home there, partly because of the huge emphasis on rugby and cricket, in which I was unable to participate.

During these teenage years, Vygeboom began to experience the phenomenon of urban creep. This was evident from the complaints made by some people from the suburb about flies attracted by the cattle and chicken manure on the farm. The farm was gradually subdivided, plots sold off and suburban houses built, and today the area is an extension of Durbanville. The old farmhouse was sold, demolished and replaced with a modern building that, I have since heard, is used as a men's club. Durbanville's majestic bluegum avenue is no more and has been replaced by a dual carriageway, with traffic lights every few hundred metres. By this time, my parents had made a home in the adjoining suburb of Valmary Park, where they spent their last years. My father died a year after Mandela was released from prison, happy to see the dawn of democracy in South Africa.

One Sunday, late in the afternoon, we had, as was the custom, dropped Marcelle at Springfield Convent, and my father was about to drop me at Krysia and Kevin's home in Newlands. As we drove through the leafy suburb of Wynberg, we were, unusually, on our own and began a rare discussion about my future studies.

'Education, education, education,' my father said, repeating his much-repeated refrain, 'they cannot take that away from you.' He then indicated that he was keen for me to go to Stellenbosch University rather than the more liberal University of Cape Town (UCT), as he was worried that I would get mixed up with 'political' students on campus.

He then announced, 'So, next year you are out of the nest!'

My heart froze. I did not say anything. I questioned him tentatively, and he agreed that he would pay the fees for my first year, but thereafter I was to fund myself.

I ended up applying to both universities but decided to accept the offer at UCT for the simple reason that I had heard of the brutal initiation rituals at Stellenbosch. These might be disastrous for a haemophiliac. I was medically exempt from the army and so, immediately after matriculating, I registered for a combined commerce and law degree. The commerce component was meant to appease my father, who would rather I study medicine, to have a ticket to leave in case things went awry in South Africa. I set about applying for bursaries and eventually accepted a civil service bursary, which required me to work for the government for an equivalent number of years. My father was happy to see me graduate with a law degree in 1976.

*

Over the years members of the vast family moved on. Some married and had children; others had children but were not married. Nephews and nieces sprang up like mushrooms. My father, who had kept a Collins Diary in his back pocket ever since I could remember, would meticulously note the birth date of every new-born grandchild, resulting in more than thirty entries before his death.

About a decade after I completed university, my father and Mom took me aside to speak about their will, which they had recently attended to. They informed me that they had drawn up a joint will so that, when one of them died, the other would inherit the deceased's half-share. My parents also informed me that they had appointed two executors: stepsister Janet, to represent the Edwards side of the family, and me on the Glazewski side.

As my father was twenty years older than my stepmother, it was very likely that he would die before her. My father specifically remarked at this meeting that, when he died, I would not immediately inherit anything, but that my share would come to me once my stepmother died. I was somewhat wary that my stepmother might change the joint will after my father died. But after her death, I discovered that my fears were completely unfounded. She remained true and fair till the end, leaving each child exactly one-fourteenth of the estate as the joint will stipulated.

After my father's death many years later, and during my working career at the University of Cape Town, I would visit Mom more or less monthly, usually for an early supper, as she was living alone in Valmary Park. Virtually all her own children had moved abroad or were living elsewhere. On these visits I noticed how frugally she lived: she would keep a poor-looking half-tomato in her fairly empty fridge, for example. I was aware that a substantial amount of money had been made from the sale of the subdivided plots, although the details were never spoken about. Over the rather strained supper conversation I would make suggestions for her to have a holiday, perhaps to visit her brother who was then living in Zimbabwe, or even to take a boat cruise. She shrugged these suggestions off with a laugh.

*

Despite my initial misgivings about my father marrying Mrs Edwards, she became the mainstay of my growing-up years. As an adult I realised that she had played a vital role for my father by giving him a new lease of life after my mother's death. Without her, he would in all probability have simply curled up and faded away.

Mom outlived my father and died in peace at her Valmary Park home in 2015. For her memorial, I composed a brief eulogy: 'Kathleen had three official names: born Morris, her maiden name, which she bore during the years that shaped her. Her mother, Granny Morris, had walked away from their Irish village to start a new life in England. Her father, Brigadier Morris, served in the colonial army in India and Rhodesia, where she was born. Later on, she was Kathleen Edwards, having married Launce, with whom she had eight children, and finally she was Kathleen Glazewska, after marrying my father Gustaw, with whom she had two more children.'

I never did deliver this eulogy, and instead said a few words off the cuff, in tribute to my remarkable stepmom.

PART 2
Lifeboats

CHAPTER 4

Education, Education, Education

FRESHER'S WEEK. I was at university at last, seated in what was then called Jameson Hall. I listened intently to the welcome address by Sir Richard Luyt, the vice chancellor and former governor of British Guiana. He surveyed us fresh-faced students, and said, 'Look to the person to the left of you, and then to the right of you. Only one of you will graduate.' I nearly pooped in my pants.

As I have mentioned, my father would have preferred that I study medicine, which could provide a ticket to leave should the fraught political situation in South Africa necessitate emigration – just as he had had to leave Poland. But I'd spent so much time in hospitals as a patient that there was no chance of my studying medicine; instead, I chose law, registering for the combined commerce–law degree, BCom LLB, rather than the more conventional arts and law degree. It seemed more transferable should I ever need to leave the country.

In my first year, particularly in my Latin class, I spent much of my time looking with fascination at the girls, simply observing, not having the social wherewithal to interact with them. Having been at all-boys' high schools and having only minimal experience of girls, I was fascinated with what they wore, their accessories – including the stickers adorning one girl's suitcase.

During this first year, I continued boarding with Krysia and Kevin and formed a close bond with six classmates who had also opted for the less popular BCom LLB. Three of them, Gus, Dave and Lindsay, are my friends to this day. Once Lindsay invited me to his Constantia home for lunch during my first term. I recall looking wide-eyed at their opulent family estate, with horse paddocks, large swimming pool and tennis court set among lush lawns and shady trees. His mother interrogated me about my background, and when she learned that I lived in Newlands with my sister and her husband, she asked which side of the railway line that would be. My response elicited a frown, as they lived on the wrong side – albeit only a stone's throw from the class-dividing railway tracks.

But I wasn't happy. University life did not seem to be what it was pumped to be. Apart from socialising with my immediate group of six classmates, it felt as if I had merely changed schools. Weekends, in particular, seemed empty. I rather tentatively applied for university residence, disclosing that I was haemophiliac. I was hesitant to do so as I'd assumed (incorrectly, as it turned out) that my delicate medical situation, combined with my inability to participate in sport and related student activities, would preclude me from living in a robust men's residence. A few months after putting in my application, I was called to the phone by Krysia. A plummy male voice asked if I was Jan Glazewski. Thinking it was a classmate fooling around, I replied in an even more exaggerated accent, 'Oh yes, how may I help you?' Then, to my horror, I realised that it was Professor Saunders, the warden of Driekoppen residence (now Kopano), offering me a place. Despite this faux pas, I was accepted, and my life was transformed – learning to play bridge, building rag floats, hoofing it down to the Pig 'n' Whistle with new friends. My 'real' university life had begun.

I also acquired my first car at that time – a powder-blue 1958 Ford Prefect, which I bought for R200 from the local garage in Durbanville, where my father was friendly with the French business owner. It looked rather out of place in the residence parking lot among the shiny, modern cars of the sons of wealthy Johannesburg parents.

Right: My *Dziadzio* (grandfather) lived in a basement flat in Lviv after World War II. Pictures of this beloved estate are visible on the wall.

Middle: The manor house before its demolition by the Russians in 1939. All that remains today is the cellar in the foreground.

Bottom: The Dniester River view from where the manor house stood before it was destroyed by the Russians in 1939.

Top left: A portrait of my father Gustaw, painted in Cairo during the war. It used to hang on the dining room wall behind the head of the table where my father sat. Today it hangs on my dining room wall.

Top right: My paternal grandmother at a young age. She died of Spanish flu in the early 1920s.

Bottom: The brothers in France, 1967. From left to right is Gustaw (my father), Kot, Ignacy and Andrzej (the mystical priest).

Top left: My mother, Helena, during World War II, in Palestine, where she worked for the Polish Red Cross.

Top right: My father was a natty dresser. Cape Town, circa 1970.

Right: My parents with their first born, Adam, in Romania after they had left Poland. Adam died in Palestine, aged three, from haemophilia-related internal bleeding.

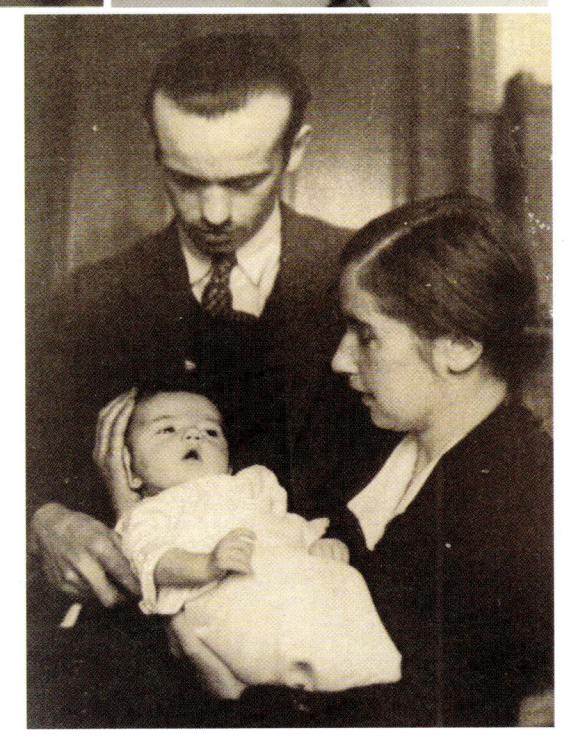

УКРАЇНА
ТЕРНОПІЛЬСЬКА ОБЛАСНА ДЕРЖАВНА
АДМІНІСТРАЦІЯ
ДЕРЖАВНИЙ АРХІВ
ТЕРНОПІЛЬСЬКОЇ ОБЛАСТІ
46000 м.Тернопіль, вул. Сагайдачного, 14
тел.(0352) 52-44-95, факс (0352) 52-26-18
e-mail: dato_bogd@ukr.net
ідент. код 03494729

UKRAINE
TERNOPIL REGIONAL STATE
ADMINISTRATION
STATE ARCHIVES
TERNOPIL REGION
46000 Ternopil, 14, Sahaidachny St.
Phones: (0352) 52-44-95, fax: (0352) 52-26-18
e-mail: dato_bogd@ukr.net

06.09. 2006р.№ Г-135

На №_____

Архівна довідка

Гр.Смольському І.Р.
вул.. Зубрівська 17 кв. 45.
м. Львів 79066

У документах «Тернопільського воєводського управління, м.Тернопіль», в списках великих землевласників Заліщицького повіту за 1939 р. числиться:

Глажевський Адам /Głażewski Adam/, власник маєтку у с.Хмільова /Chmielowa/. Площа маєтку 326 га.

Підстава: ДАТО,ф.231,оп.6,спр.2737,арк. 16зв.

Директор   Б.Хаварівський

Above: Official letter verifying that my grandfather, Adam, was the owner of 326 ra. (hectares) in Chmielowa, Poland. I tried to pursue a land claim without success.

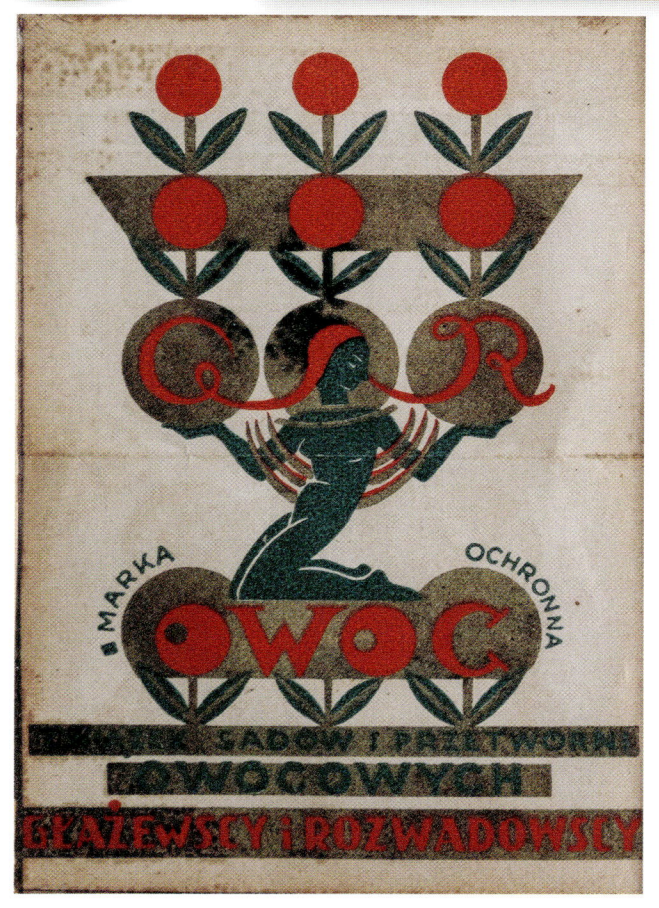

Above: Wine labels from Chmielowa, my grandfather's estate. My father, who studied horticulture in France, was the first person in Poland to grow and bottle his own wine.

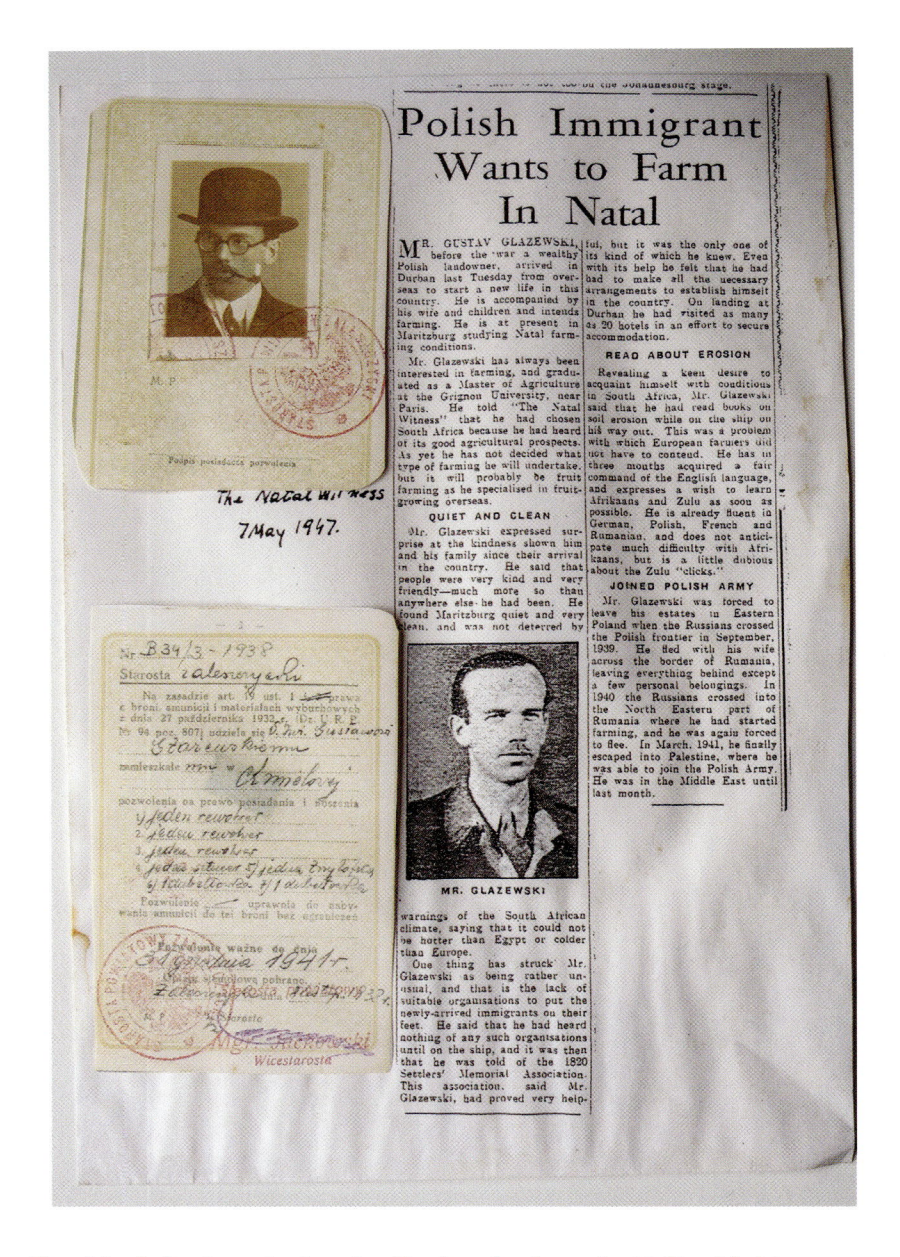

Top: My father's arrival at the Durban harbour in 1947 with his young family (my three older sisters) was newsworthy enough to be reported on in *The Natal Witness*.

Left: Cotswold farmhouse, where I spent my childhood.

Left: Me on the stoep at Cotswold farm, circa 1960.

Left: With my childhood friends on Cotswold farm, where I started thinking out of the box.

Above: Looking saintly at my first Holy Communion (centre with stepbrother John on my left).

Bottom: Childhood friend Kuba Miszewski and I kicked soccer balls around in 1960 and still do so today.

My father was correct in his concerns about the politically active UCT students. During the early 1970s there were numerous student demonstrations. I was shocked to witness the police violence when they brutally broke up a peaceful student protest on Jameson steps. I cowered away and watched from the third floor of the adjoining Jagger Library. One baton blow on the head would probably have been the end of me. My elder, politically active stepsister Mary was completing her studies at the time, and encouraged me to join the National Union of South African Students (Nusas), a left-wing, anti-apartheid student organisation. But I knew no one there personally, and was afraid that if I, an outsider, attended a meeting, I might be labelled a spy.

*

It was during my second year at UCT, and while I was back home at Vygeboom during the university holiday, that my father received news from England that his brother Andrzej (my uncle Andrew, the 'mystical priest') had died of a heart attack. I was always intrigued by reports of his extraordinary esoteric talents. On hearing of his death I decided I should visit faraway Europe to meet my distant relatives, most of whom were locked away in communist Poland, and about whom I had only heard stories. At that time, special reduced-cost student flights were available through Sabena airline.

Serendipitously, my happy-go-lucky residence friend Kevin was also keen to visit Europe. He often missed early-morning lectures and borrowed my lecture notes – to my chagrin, doing better than conscientious I did in the mid-year tests. So it was that the two of us boarded the cheap Sabena flight (a mere R310 return, if I remember correctly) to London via Luxembourg during the summer of 1973–1974. It was my first experience of Europe and of a real winter. I happily forfeited the long summer holiday in South Africa.

*

Kevin and I – at the time dishevelled, long-haired students – landed at Heathrow from Luxembourg and caught a red bus into London, as the Piccadilly line had not yet been extended to the airport. While Kevin went to visit an uncle in Brighton, my first taste of London was the few days I spent with my stepsister Margie, who was staying in a squat at the time. While walking down to the local store to buy something for supper, she coolly asked me if I would like to try some acid. I nearly fell over from the shock, but kept my composure, saying: 'Not right now, thanks.'

Kevin and I hooked up again to visit the Continent. We both had a Eurail pass, slept on trains, and spent time taking in the sights. In Rome I was moved by our visit to the Roman Forum, which had occupied a central place in my school Latin classes, as well as the Colosseum, which a passing American recommended seeing, as 'it was free'. In Paris, Kevin and I were openly accosted by some ladies of the night in Pigalle, a novel experience for us both, coming as we did from a repressed Calvinist society. In a German beerhall, I remember learning drinking songs in that language but no longer know which town that was in.

Then I split from Kevin again to visit more family members. The first port of call was my French family. First was my father's brother Kot and his wife, *Ciocia* Joanna, in their opulent apartment near Versailles. They also owned a chateau in the country. It was evident that they were still living in pre-war Poland, hoping that the motherland would someday be restored to its former status. My uncle and aunt seemed reluctant to put me in touch with the youngest of their five children, Jojo (Jolante) and Dominik, who were more or less my contemporaries. Prior to my trip I'd learned from Kot's letters to my father that the two were 'problem children' – Jojo had run away from school and got mixed up with left-leaning friends – and Kot was tearing his hair out because of their various escapades. But when, soon afterwards, I met these two cousins, living on a barge on the Seine, they seemed completely normal to me. Jojo immediately became something of a sister to me, and we remain close friends to this day, sharing, among other things, our interest in our paternal fathers' ancestral roots.

A week or two later, I joined the whole family, excluding the two black sheep, at the family chateau in Burgundy for a weekend visit. There I met three other cousins, including the eldest, Michał, and his newly wed wife, Natalie. After a sumptuous Sunday lunch, I was asked if I would like a second helping. Trying to parade my limited knowledge of French, I replied, 'Non merci, je suis pleine' (No, thank you, I am pregnant) to peals of laughter. I felt immediately at home with my new-found family. In subsequent years I was to spend many pleasant summers and Christmas visits with Michał and Natalie at their hospitable home in northern Provence.

Soon after meeting my French relations, I ventured into Poland for the first time.

*

It was 1973–1974, and South African passports were then stamped with the permission to enter 'all countries except...', followed by a long list of African and Communist bloc countries. So I had to obtain a letter of invitation from a Polish relative, plus a special endorsement from the South African government, to visit my relatives. I was rather cavalier about travelling freely on buses and trains, as I'd brought along from South Africa only a limited supply of my blood-clotting factor and had by then used it all up. I had only managed to squeeze about ten boxes of it into my luggage – in those days, factor VIII was bulky, and I had to administer it through a 50 ml drip.

I left Kevin in Zurich and headed to Poland. My journey necessitated changing trains at Friedrichstrasse, located in former East Berlin, and undergoing strenuous border scrutiny. The officials regarded my South African passport with great suspicion. Nevertheless, I boarded the Warsaw train, and after an hour I was at last in Poland. The atmosphere changed immediately as we crossed the border, both inside the six-berth compartment and outside the train window, where the grey landscape was gradually transformed from drab to austere in the dull light. Inside, my fellow travellers seemed to be returning from a visit to the West to stock up on food, which was tucked away in shiny plastic bags. After some small talk with my immediate neighbour, everybody in the compartment immediately perked up when it became clear from my rudimentary Polish that I was a foreigner. They were even more intrigued when they discovered that I was 'from Africa', and not black. I was offered thickly sliced egg sandwiches and gulps of bottled water, and I felt that at last I was among my people.

But then I asked, 'How is life under the communist government?'

It was as if I had turned off the lights. Everyone sat up straight immediately, shuffled their feet, stared straight ahead, and not another word was uttered. The conversation – and bonhomie – was over.

Over a decade later, while I was a postgraduate student at the London School of Economics, I made the same trip to Poland. This time I boarded the Warsaw-bound train from Amsterdam. But at the same border at Friedrichstrasse in Berlin, the train ground to an ominous halt. While East German military probed the underside of the train with bayonets, two seemingly seven-foot-tall customs officials entered my shared compartment to check documentation. As before, my South African passport included the stamp prohibiting travel to Eastern bloc countries, though I had again obtained the necessary invitation and endorsement permitting travel to Poland and transit through East Germany. 'Ra-ceeest!' a blue-uniformed giant bellowed at me. Worse was to follow. The two proceeded to ransack my hand luggage, where they found several bottles marked factor VIII, containing a white powdery substance. Ignoring my protestations and my haemophilia travel card, they frog-marched me to a small chilly office on the platform where I had to strip to my underpants while they took a bottle of my medication for verification. Still worse was to follow. On stripping me, they found a US$20 note that I had slipped into my shoe. As one was obliged to exchange US dollars at a fixed rate for the duration of one's stay in Poland, I had been advised to take extra dollars, for one could obtain ten times more on the black market.

'Please, I have a train to catch,' I protested, trembling.

'Zug weg [Train gone],' was the terse reply.

After endless hours, my precious bottles of factor VIII were returned – one, however, was opened and thus unusable. I was released and told to wait for the next connecting train to Warsaw, which was scheduled to arrive eight hours later. I was unable to muster any enthusiasm to use the time for a little sightseeing in East Berlin, so instead I sat on a cold hard bench on the wintry platform. After careful deliberation, I warily offered the uniformed Russian army officer sitting next to me a Marlboro cigarette, which he accepted with a grunt.

*

To return to my first trip to Poland in December 1973 while I was a student: I was met at Warsaw's Rynek Główny (main station) by my late mother's half-sister, *Ciocia* Lula Bojanowska, and her two teenage sons. We took a tram to their airless apartment where her husband, *Wuj* Maciej, sat snuggled in a dressing gown and slippers. The small flat was jam-packed with furniture, and a bed had been unhooked from the lounge wall for my use. I was struck by the small living spaces in Europe generally, but in Poland in particular.

Later that evening, *Wuj* Maciej informed me that he was an English teacher, and he showed off his linguistic prowess. However, he had obviously learned English from reading, as his rather odd pronunciation demonstrated, as he had no access to listening devices. He would, for instance, accentuate the final syllable of words in this way: 'It was the most terr-*ible* cas-*tle* imagin-*able*.'

An intense social programme awaited the long-lost cousin from Africa. I was exhausted after the train journey from Zurich, but *Ciocia* Lula had arranged a party to welcome the returning cousin that first evening. About thirty guests were squeezed shoulder-to-shoulder in the cramped confines of the lounge, quaffing the traditional Polish welcome drink of neat vodka, customarily served with herring. I was bombarded with endless questions: 'How is the weather in Africa?'; 'Do you know my friend, a fine Pole who lives in Sudan?'; 'Aren't all the people black there?' An elderly gentleman asked me whether I enjoyed hunting in Africa, informing me that my grandfather had been 'a great wild boar hunter'. When I responded that I did not participate in that 'sport', he walked away to pour himself another drink.

The next night, I was subjected to a Polish version of Shakespeare's *The Tempest* in the State Theatre, not a word of which I could understand, and so I could barely keep my eyes open. That day, *Ciocia* Lula had shown me an interminable series of photographs of distant unknown aunts and uncles, and then put me through an endless account of her own visit to my mother, her half-sister in Africa, entailing no fewer than eight stops before her arrival at Cotswold farm when I was still a toddler. She hauled out a dog-eared South African Airways breakfast menu, which included an offering of 'traditional pap'.

After a few days in Warsaw, it was with some relief that I was able to announce that I wanted to make arrangements to visit my mother's biological sister, *Ciocia* Wanda Wiktor, in Gdynia. Wiktor was their maiden name, but *Ciocia* Wanda had married someone also called Wiktor, and so her surname hadn't changed. *Ciocia* Lula offered to dial the number for me, but to my surprise, at the sound of the ring tone, she thrust the handset into my hand, saying, 'You speak!' I learned later that the two sisters had not communicated since the war: *Ciocia* Lula had apparently appropriated most of the family furniture and portraits from my maternal grandfather's manor house located at Zarszyn, in southeastern Poland. My widowed grandfather had married a second time, and Lula was his daughter from the second marriage. As I knew from my own experience, second marriages can complicate existing family relationships.

As the train slowed into Gdynia station, it was accompanied by a rolling evening mist or, more accurately, a fog largely consisting of industrial pollution. Gathering together my rucksack and other belongings, I stacked them in the corridor as other passengers were doing. I looked anxiously out of the window at the large crowd on the platform.

'How will I recognise you?' I had asked *Ciocia* Wanda, in my very limited Polish, when I phoned her from Warsaw.

'Oh! You will!'

I understood what she meant, even though I was still struggling to express myself in the language of my childhood. As I peered through the foggy haze at the station, a replica of my mother appeared, and my stomach fluttered.

'Janek,' she chuckled in my mother's voice. My heart stopped. I scrambled off the train, gave her an awkward hug, and we set off for her home.

I spent the next few days in her tiny flat, struggling to communicate, as my Polish had hardly been used since I was nine when my father remarried. He and I spoke only English in our new South African family. *Ciocia* Wanda could not speak a word of English, but I revelled in the familiar tones of her voice as she mended my clothes and sewed on some buttons for me – just as my mother would have done. At that time I was having severe internal elbow bleeds and had run out of the bulky factor VIII that I had brought with me. Thankfully, *Ciocia* Wanda managed to secure some factor VIII for me through her medical connections, and my elbow settled down.

On about the third evening, she said, 'A youngster like you should not just be sitting around my flat.' But for me, this was far more enjoyable than swilling beer in German beerhalls or camping in some youth hostel in rural Switzerland. Kevin and I had explored several countries, often spending the night on the train to save the cost of an inhospitable foreign hostel. But here, in this cosy Polish living room, I felt at home.

That evening in Gdynia, sitting on *Ciocia* Wanda's easy chair near her gas heater, Polish words I never thought I knew came tumbling out. It was as if I had opened an old box in my head: I can speak Polish! In the days that followed, people would often laugh – a 20-year-old speaking like a 6-year-old child, with the added fascination of my father's pre-war accent. I had an urge to stay in Poland, and vowed I would take a year off from my studies to spend time there, but instead I got caught up in the hurly-burly of my South African life. I have never carried out this promise to myself – which, to this day, I hold dear.

The most intense memory I have of that visit is Christmas Eve at *Ciocia* Wanda's flat, when we sang the same Christmas carols that I had sung as a child at Cotswold farm with my parents and sisters. This brought a lump to my throat, as the singing of Polish carols had gradually petered out during the Vygeboom years.

I was surprised when, on the day after Christmas – known in South Africa as Boxing Day, a time for socialising and having a good party – *Ciocia* Wanda announced after a simple breakfast of scrambled eggs that we would all be going to Mass. What surprised me even more was that the church was as packed as if it had been Christmas Eve. I later learned from *Ciocia* Wanda that this particular church had been built surreptitiously in a barn, literally undercover, to hide its existence from the communist regime. And so, the crowded church was partly a display of solidarity against the government.

Little did I know that, a decade later, history would be made when the Catholic Church, with its strong following in Poland – boosted by the election in 1989 of John Paul II, the first non-Italian pope in four centuries, and a Pole to boot – would play a key role in overthrowing communism. This was achieved in collaboration with the Solidarity trade union movement under the leadership of Lech Wałesa, the 1983 Nobel Peace Prize laureate, who became president of Poland in 1990. On a later visit to Poland, *Ciocia* Wanda pointed out the former trade unionist's washing line, which was just visible from her tiny balcony. On Monday mornings his laundry could be seen hanging in the frosty winter air or flapping in the summer breeze.

Back in Warsaw, I visited distant relatives on my mother's side, the Serwatowskis. I trudged along muddy alleys at five in the afternoon when it was already dark, past endless identical high-rise flats – Stalin blocks, as they were known. The long, cold walk contrasted with the warm reception I received after walking up to the fourteenth floor that evening. 'Here is your bed,' my relatives said in welcome. Rather disconcertingly, they regarded me as a prodigal son from Africa, with Poland, not South Africa, being my home.

During that first three-week trip to Poland, I also contacted Therese Rozwadowska, who was part of the generation of Poles I had grown up with in South Africa. She was an art student in the historic city of Cracow. It was wonderful to connect with someone who, like me, felt half Polish and half South African. Later, I was to learn that many Polish South Africans with whom I had grown up felt similarly, occupying a national no-man's land. I recollect Therese describing how she had just spent time with an elderly relative whose legs were paralysed as a result of being tortured during the Stalin era, when he was made to stand in knee-deep water in his cell both day and night. The story stayed with me, probably as I had heard of similar methods meted out to detainees in South Africa under apartheid's so-called anti-terrorism laws.

Cracow was extremely polluted at the time owing to Stalin's decision to locate a steel smelting plant on the outskirts. This, I was told, was to punish Cracovians for showing insufficient enthusiasm for Soviet communism.

This was my first trip to Poland and my first encounter with bleak urban winter landscapes, with snow and intense cold. But what struck me most was the contrast with the warmth and the deep sense of culture that I experienced from welcoming relatives and others whom I met. A profound connection with my family and my ancestral roots had been established, and I vowed to come back.

*

During my final year of university, 1976, Soweto erupted, making me and many of my classmates – especially those who had yet to do military service – consider emigration. I was aghast at the police brutality, reports of which filtered through the news networks, and shocked at the reaction of some of my classmates who felt that the riots were caused by 'troublemakers' and should immediately be quelled.

Soon afterwards, I received a letter from the civil service informing me that, immediately after graduating, I was to report to the legal department of the head office of the Receiver of Revenue in Pretoria to fulfil my bursary obligation. Other colleagues were to work for the Department of Justice, but because I had done a combined law and commerce degree rather than the conventional law and arts degree, I was shunted to the revenue department. The letter directed me to report to the head office in Pretoria on the first working day of January 1977. My career was about to begin.

CHAPTER 5

My Blossoming Career

AFTER GRADUATING in December 1976, I looked forward with some trepidation to my new life in Pretoria in the new year. With my savings, I bought a good, second-hand, again coincidentally a powder-blue Volkswagen Beetle and phoned a few friends to say goodbye. One of these was my UCT classmate, John M. It turned out that he and his girlfriend, Jo, needed a lift to Johannesburg for a job interview. The couple were dropped off at Vygeboom by Jo's sister, Trish. Off we whizzed up the N1, John and I embarking on our new careers, no longer carefree students it seemed.

As we approached the unfamiliar city of Johannesburg, I gaily said to John, 'It's New Year's Eve. What do you think we should do?'

In typical John style, he said, 'There's a party I know about – at Fourways.'

'I'll meet you there later,' I said, getting some sketchy directions as I dropped him off in a Joburg suburb before heading for Pretoria. I had arranged with a friend of my sister Marysia to stay in a converted garage at the home of her university friend Betty, then married to Martin Welz, who would later become the founding editor of the investigative magazine *Noseweek*. I would on occasion meet Martin for lunch, and he would pick my brains for newsworthy stories emanating from the revenue department.

I got lost on the way back to Fourways but eventually located the party, where I knew no one except John. But in the course of the evening I found myself chatting to a genial middle-aged woman, Jo S. She mentioned that she and her husband lived in Pretoria, and invited the 'new boy' in town to come around sometime, an offer I took up with alacrity, joining them the following Sunday for lunch. I had many convivial Sunday braais with them and their three sons, including Paul S, who was living in Johannesburg at the time and studying law part-time. A few years later I shared a communal house with him and others in Melville while I was doing my law articles. Some three years later, I was extremely touched when Paul and his wife named their first-born son Janek, the Polish diminutive of my name. It was at this time that, through Paul, I again met Trish and her soon-to-be husband, who had in the meantime moved to Johannesburg. This group formed the core of my Johannesburg social circle. We remain firm friends to this day.

A few of my ex-university classmates also ended up in Pretoria, either because they had similar bursaries and were working as prosecutors for the Department of Justice or because they had been summoned to do their compulsory military service in Pretoria. It was comforting to have a cohort of former classmates with me in my newly adopted town, and to host them on weekends, when we had some memorable wild parties.

One of the unexpected advantages of living in the predominantly conservative, Afrikaans environment of Pretoria was that if one met an English speaker, one formed an immediate connection. One of the few English speakers in the Special Tax Court Office was the elderly court stenographer, Gwen, who introduced me to her daughter Gail, then a student at Rhodes University. Along with my housemate Brian, we set out to acquaint ourselves with the local nightlife and the music spots – which did not take longer than a week. Our favourite hangout was a nightclub in central Pretoria, where the Silver Creek Mountain Band played.

Work began sharp at eight. If you did not pitch up on time, there would be a black mark next to your name. But if I happened to read the morning paper for half an hour or so after eight, that was fine. I would arrive with the liberal *Rand Daily Mail*, which raised eyebrows among my work colleagues – they dubbed it 'The Daily Wail'. Morning tea was at ten, and it was compulsory for the half-dozen or so legal staff of the Special Tax Court – all Afrikaans-speaking men, most of whom had seemingly not made it as lawyers in private practice – to congregate in the windowless tea room for some tepid tea. One was meant to discuss tax law matters, but in reality the conversation always turned either to rugby or to politics. The United States came in for much flak, in particular because of President Jimmy Carter's vehement opposition to South Africa's apartheid policies. I was always on the back foot in these discussions, as I unsuccessfully attempted to promote the liberal cause. It was during this time that I learned that political views, like religion, are seemingly embedded in people's psyche, and, try as one might, argument or persuasion usually can't change an antagonist's views. I merely succeeded in alienating myself from the rest of the staff, and I made not an iota of difference to their ideas about apartheid.

I did slightly better on Fridays, when the conversation was inevitably about the next day's rugby match and the chances of Northern Transvaal (later, the Blue Bulls). There I could hold my own, and even had a chance of winning the office lottery by predicting the final score.

The best part of my working day was lunchtime, when I strode off to the Burlington Arcade to join a group of journalists from various English newspapers, including the *Pretoria News* and *Rand Daily Mail*. We would gather at the outside tables of the busy arcade for midday lunch and conversation. I felt much more among my own, at home at least for forty-five minutes of the day. Here I learned first-hand of the brutal death in detention of Steve Biko on the day it happened, and later about his huge funeral service in the Eastern Cape and the stifled anger felt among the masses – details one did not read about in the media.

I befriended one of these journalists, Muff Andersson, who seemed inordinately keen to get to know me, albeit not in a romantic way. She was the music reviewer for the Argus group of newspapers and would pass on to me some of the LP records she had reviewed. My favourites were the early Joan Armatrading albums, in particular the song 'Love and Affection'. A month or so into our friendship, Muff drew me aside and asked if I would be prepared to assist the ANC in exile to smuggle weapons into South Africa across the Botswana border. While I was sympathetic to the cause, the thought of possibly being detained and physically assaulted by the security police scared the living daylights out of me, so I politely refused.

A mistake I made while working in the Special Tax Court Office was to sneak off for an hour or so during office hours to attend the Biko inquest, which took place in the former Jewish synagogue up the road. I was riveted by the performance of Sydney Kentridge, one of South Africa's top advocates at the time, and father of the renowned artist William Kentridge. Someone in the office snitched on me, and I was severely rapped on the knuckles. The inquest verdict, that no one could be held responsible for Biko's death in custody, effectively exculpated the security police. Kentridge would leave South Africa shortly thereafter to commence a stellar practice in London.

I took a vacation during this time with my girlfriend, Lita, an archaeologist whom I met at the bus stop on my daily commute to work, and a university friend, Rory, to do some hiking and exploring on the Transkei coast. We happened to bump into a varsity colleague, Neil, who was on honeymoon at the time with his English wife. I mentioned to him that I was dissatisfied with my job in the civil service. He asked me what I'd really like to do. As if from nowhere, a voice replied, 'Write a book on environmental law.' Quite an odd thing for me to say in 1978, as the discipline of environmental law was then non-existent, at least in South Africa. Moreover, I had never articulated this sentiment before, not even half-jokingly, as I did then.

I decided that I had to move on from the civil service, which seemed to hold no future for me, and possibly even to emigrate. I applied for a bursary to do a master's degree abroad and was accepted at the London School of Economics (LSE), again to my father's consternation. Soon afterwards, I was tempted to take up an offer to join the *Rand Daily Mail* as a cadet journalist. After some hesitation, I decided on the London option for a master's degree in law, as I felt it might open up overseas career possibilities.

Having worked off my debt to the civil service, I left the Receiver of Revenue and headed for London to do the master's at LSE. While there, I was a frequent visitor at the home of *Ciocia* Ala, who had left South Africa and settled in Ealing, where every second person in the street seemed Polish, as I discovered when asking for directions to the local travel agent or bank. I recollect her crying out with joy, 'Papierz jest Polak' (the Pope is Polish), when it was announced that Karol Wojtyła had been elected as head of the Catholic Church. While in London, I took the opportunity once again to visit Poland, in particular *Ciocia* Wanda, my late mother's sister, whose spark and vivaciousness seemed by then to have dissipated. This was the last time I saw her. I was very sad when her daughter let me know that she had died. She was the last direct link to my late mother.

*

Soon after returning to South Africa I took up employment as an articled clerk in 1981 with Bell Dewar and Hall, a progressive law firm in Johannesburg that had a 'struggle face' as well as a 'commercial law face'. The senior partner was Kelsey Stuart, a leading media lawyer who had taken on the responsibility of acting for the *Rand Daily Mail* after its exposé of the Info Scandal, following which it was besieged by the apartheid state for criticising the regime and exposing the brutalities of apartheid. One day, after I'd been a year or so at the firm, Mr Stuart walked past my open office door after his customary lunch break and gave his usual nod of greeting. Half an hour later, he died of a severe stroke, aged 52. I intuitively knew it was stress-related. Soon thereafter, government pressure forced the shutdown of the *Rand Daily Mail* – a watershed event marking the end of an era of liberal journalism in mainline newspapers though it ushered in a period of struggle newspapers such as the *Weekly Mail* (now the *Mail & Guardian*) and *Vrye Weekblad*.

The mid-1980s saw increasing resistance and anger mounting against the apartheid regime. Shortly before I left my Pretoria job a car bomb went off in central Pretoria, killing nearly twenty civilians. Bell Dewar and Hall was involved in a number of political cases, including the Neil Aggett inquest in 1982. The medical doctor and trade unionist was alleged to have hanged himself in a police cell at John Vorster Square after having been detained. He was the first white person to die in these circumstances. Bell Dewar and Hall acted as the attorneys for the Aggett family at the inquest, where they argued that indefinite detention was a form of torture, illegal under international law. The next few years would see an increased number of demonstrations and strikes, as well as numerous detentions without trial, and a series of states of emergency declared under President PW Botha.

The 1980s was a tumultuous time in Eastern Europe, too, in particular in Poland. The trade union Solidarity had come into being there in 1980, and by the end of the decade the Berlin Wall had fallen. A call for liberation from the oppressive communist regime swept through Poland and Eastern Europe. I wondered how my cousins in Poland were doing. I felt I should be involved in helping them in some way, but I was too preoccupied at the time to do so.

A few months after completing my articles in Johannesburg, I realised that the hurly-burly of legal practice in the commercial heart

My Blossoming Career

of the country was not for me. I had made many friends and had a great social life but decided to move back to Cape Town. My intention was to join a Cape Town law firm and take the conveyancing and notarial exams in order to practise land law. But I coincidentally learned that an international auditing firm was looking for junior staff in its tax division in Cape Town. I used this opportunity as my ticket back to Cape Town.

On my return, I put out word that I was looking for accommodation, once again through John M. He had heard of a cottage in Mowbray going for rent as the tenant had recently lost her husband. During the interview, I met the deceased man's sister Liz and was immediately attracted to her. We ended up having a long-term relationship.

Liz, a journalist, encouraged me to accompany her to the historic launch of the United Democratic Front (UDF) in Mitchells Plain. It was 20 August 1983, and close to ten thousand people attended the event. A number of political activists, including Trevor Manuel, were elected to the leadership of the UDF that evening. Many ended up holding key positions in the new democratic South African government that came to power in 1994.

Another thing I did on my return was to reinstate my relationship with the Haematology Department at Groote Schuur Hospital. I was assigned to a recently qualified physician, Dr Mike du Toit. At our first consultation, he promised to deliver my factor VIII to my home in nearby Mowbray after he finished work. I knew immediately that here was a special doctor and we remain friends to this day.

I began commuting daily to work, in a suit and tie, on the eighteenth floor of Shell House in central Cape Town, where I was employed by the accounting firm Arthur Andersen. Here I tried to fit into the mould of an aspiring tax lawyer, but it just did not seem to be the real me. I was aware at the time of an environmental master's degree by course work in the School of Environmental Studies at UCT. Some non-law friends from my UCT days spoke highly of the course, in particular of its interdisciplinary aspect.

With the encouragement of Liz, I decided to have an exploratory talk with the head of the unit, Professor Richard Fuggle. It was early February 1984, and I remember arriving early at his secretary's office overlooking University Avenue, and bumping into a charming, outgoing man, John Raimondo, in the lobby. He told me that he had been a successful businessman who decided to give up the corporate life, and he said how happy he was doing the degree.

My interest was certainly piqued during the meeting with Professor Fuggle. He told me that the new academic year would commence at the end of that month with a field trip to Cape Point, and that there was a place for me should I wish to register for the master's degree. I was sorely tempted but at the same time hesitant, as this was way off my career path at that time. I noticed a shiny red book on his desk and learned that he and Professor André Rabie had recently co-edited a pioneering multidisciplinary work titled *Environmental Concerns in South Africa*. I went out and bought it.

To allay my concerns, I visited Guy, a friend from university days who had completed the course, for advice. While listening to him, I was distracted by his waterless fish tank filled with red sand. I discerned some beetles scratching around. He explained that the beetles came from the sand dunes of arid Namibia and had runners down their sides to capture the moisture that came off the early morning sea mist. He had learned about this on one of the field trips. I instantly decided to take up the course. To his day, Guy believes that it was his good advice, and not the Namibian beetles, that led to this lifelong career change.

Next day, I went to my superior at Arthur Andersen and resigned, giving two weeks' notice instead of the customary month. This would enable me to join the introductory week-long field trip scheduled for the end of that month at Cape Point Nature Reserve.

Once registered for the course, I revelled in learning about local ecology, the regional fauna and flora, geology and more. On the first Monday morning, en route to Cape Point, we stopped to muck around in the rock pools past Simonstown and learn about coastal ecology. I let out a whoop of joy, realising that just two weeks earlier I had been sitting in a grey city office in a work suit and tie.

At the outset, I was nervous, knowing little about natural systems and being under the impression that the majority of the small class of six students were natural scientists. On our first field trip to Cape Point Nature Reserve, we were confronted by the bespectacled, bearded ecology professor, John Grindley, who asked the student group to identify an innocuous-looking green bush. Not even the natural science students knew its name, which the professor identified as the common blombos or *Metalasia muricata*. I took the opportunity to make my mark by informing the professor that I had studied Latin (a compulsory subject in my law degree), which seemed to impress him. Many years later I learned that the two professors, Fuggle and Grindley, had intense discussions about whether they should take a haemophiliac on board, as the course included outdoor field trips – the aspect of the course I enjoyed most.

That year, I was asked numerous legal questions by my fellow class members. Why can a developer be allowed to do this or that? Who is responsible for clean-up and liable for damage caused by an oil spill on our coastline? Of course, we were talking about environmental law, which was not yet a recognised subject in any law faculty in South Africa. I had, in the meantime, bought the Fuggle and Rabie book. Each chapter was about an aspect of natural resource management, though I noted that over half of the chapters had a legal component by Rabie. Until then, any notion of South African environmental law was a mirage, but the seed of environmental law as a legal discipline in its own right had been sown.

In the second year of the course I wrote the mini-thesis component of the degree, harnessing my revenue law background to do a study titled 'Conservation of Private Land by Means of Compensatory Mechanisms and Incentives'. It was a neat combination of my awakening passion for the nascent discipline of environmental law and my experience of fiscal law gained in Pretoria. At the same time, I started thinking about approaching local law firms for possible job opportunities once I graduated.

But then a life-changing blow was struck.

CHAPTER 6

Four Years to Live

IT WAS January 1985, and I had started writing the mini-dissertation component of my master's degree, having completed the course work the previous year. I was sharing office space with fellow master's students in a sandstone building on University Avenue at UCT.

By this time my relationship with Liz was on a firm footing. We had both been reading in the popular press about the spread of a strange new disease affecting the three Hs: homosexuals, Haitians and haemophiliacs. Later, a fourth H was added: heroin addicts. I'd heard something through the local haemophilia network about contaminated blood products imported from the United States. So, with the encouragement of Liz, I decided, for peace of mind, to go and have myself tested at Tygerberg Hospital – the only place where the blood test was available.

It was a dusty, sultry summer day in Cape Town. The gusty southeaster was blowing in from the Cape Flats. My anxiety was aggravated by the traffic lights, which seemed purposely to hold me up as I passed through Epping Industria. I felt alone. Where exactly was the pathology lab, which was supposed to be next to the sprawling Tygerberg Hospital? I was told one couldn't miss it – a tall, multi-storey face-brick building next to the hospital. 'That must be it,' I muttered to myself, but I pulled my yellow Ford Escort into the wrong parking lot and had to reverse and try all over again.

Eventually I found a bay, though it wasn't close to the lab, and had to walk, painfully, my ankle joint giving trouble again, across the sprawling parking lot with its empty cars baking in the sun. I thought about the blood products I'd received all my life and wondered what toxic substances might have been injected into me. The tall impersonal building, with its window panes gleaming in the sun, caused me to squint.

Dr Slabbert of the UCT Student Health office had told me a few days before that it would be better to fetch the blood test results myself rather than get them from him, as originally arranged. Why didn't he stick to the original plan, and give me the results himself? was the question that arose from the dark pit of my stomach. It would, after all, have been much more convenient and saved me the long drive to Tygerberg. I had been told to see a Dr Bekker – not Professor Wally Bekker, who had been quoted in the press recently about the ominous 'HTLV3 virus', as the HI virus was then called, but his recently qualified son, the head of the pathology lab.

I arrive and walk through the front entrance, trying to ignore the gnawing, tightening knot in my stomach. The lobby of the Pathology Laboratory building seems ominously quiet as I enter with some dread. The tiled floor is freshly polished, shining and sterile. I step into one of three empty lifts and step out on the eighth floor. I note that I am uncharacteristically on time and that my heart is thumping. What is the room number?

A white-coated doctor appears almost immediately at the door opposite the lift.

'Jan Glazeeeeew—?' He cannot pronounce my surname.

I glance behind him, down the long corridor. 'Gluh-*zef*-ski,' I hesitatingly correct him.

'You have AIDS,' he says.

I stare at the cold smooth quartz tiles at the base of the hard facebrick walls. I confront the deep-down intuition I've always had that the life-giving blood-clotting product would one day come back to haunt me. I am contaminated.

'What do you mean?' I ask after a pause.

He elaborates: 'AIDS is a scourge which will sweep across Africa. I am emigrating to the United States next month.'

Summoning the deep need I have for intellectual understanding, I ask, 'How does the immune system work? Explain to me the implications.'

Dr Bekker scurries back into his office, and for a minute I am left bewildered in the lift lobby area. He returns with a thick medical textbook titled *Immunology*, filled with glossy pages and diagrams. 'I will need this book back,' he says to me. Some twenty years later I will find it unopened and unread on my bookshelf, and will throw it away.

As I trudge across the sultry parking lot, I wonder what Liz's reaction will be. Will any woman ever sleep with me again? Will I still be able to play with my dear friend Trish's kids? Maybe she and her husband won't want me eating off their dinner plates. As I weave my way through the cars baking in the heat, I am surprised by a friendly 'Hello, what are you doing here?'

This startling question comes from Chris Erasmus, medical reporter for the *Cape Times* and a colleague of Liz. I grope for an answer and mouth, 'Just a regular check-up,' and then scuttle away. 'He must know!' I tremble. Did he follow me? Will there be a report in the newspaper tomorrow?

I feel shell-shocked. I get back into my car and drive slowly back to UCT – there is seemingly nothing else that I can do. I shuffle back to my desk and sit down, mumbling to my classmate Bruce, 'I have AIDS.' I am not sure whether he hears me because he does not react, and we never mention it again...

After my diagnosis I found I was not able to tell anybody apart from those closest to me: Liz, my parents and one or two close friends. Having the HTLV3 virus was a huge stigma in those early days of the epidemic. Not only was one associated with gays, who were in those homophobic years generally looked down on, but most people held the view that one could contract AIDS simply by touching an infected person. I remembered an article to which my father had recently pointed me in *Time* magazine, reporting that the home of two haemophiliac brothers had been burned down in a Southern state of the US because one of them had this new disease.

Sometime later, I bumped into Dr Gary Maartens, an immunologist at Groote Schuur Hospital, one of the bright young doctors who'd taken an interest in the disease and who had recently been appointed to head up a new HIV unit.

'Gary, tell me straight, how long have I got to live?'

'How old are you?' he asked.

'Thirty-three,' I replied.

'According to statistics, you have about four years to live,' he responded matter-of-factly. (Yet here I am, writing this almost forty years later. I often ask myself why I have survived while so many around me died at that time.)

Two important points struck me in the emotionally tumultuous days and weeks that followed the blood tests. For one thing, I should not have children, something I'd always envisaged I would do. Dreams of sitting at a table enjoying a Sunday lunch with a bunch of lively kids evaporated into thin air. Secondly, I must make the best of the time that I had. I started looking with greater intensity at the beauty of the mountain as I motored along Edinburgh Drive. I accepted invitations with alacrity, say for a Sunday drive up the West Coast to view the annual flowers – there might not be another chance.

I'd always had difficulty with personal commitments, and the diagnosis was to complicate my relationship with Liz. I would push her away emotionally and then pull her back in. After a year or two, she moved out of the house we were living in and we drifted apart, though we are still close friends to this day.

My personal feelings of loneliness, helplessness and depression were exacerbated by the partial State of Emergency declared by President Botha in July 1985. Around that time I remembered that a friend, Buzzy, had confided in me during our university days that he was bisexual. I'd heard that he was now living in London and working in an AIDS hospice as a carer for dying patients. I contacted him, and he kindly provided me with a mine of information, including the names of organisations such as London Lighthouse, a charity that supported AIDS patients, which Princess Diana would subsequently visit. But the really important introduction Buzzy gave me was to Caddie Khadeboux, an HIV-positive haemophiliac whose name he obtained from the London Haemophilia Centre. Caddie and I would become firm friends, and I would visit him and his wife whenever I was in London. Later he came to visit me while I was working in Namibia.

I continued working on my environmental master's dissertation, though with less inclination to approach law firms for a career in legal practice. But then an unexpected, life-changing job opportunity cropped up.

A UCT Law Faculty advertisement crossed my desk, for a research officer in the Institute of Marine Law. It did not particularly interest me, as marine law entails the governing regime for the high seas. However, on impulse, I decided to pop in at the office of the incumbent, a law colleague, to say farewell. Recently married, she had resigned and was moving to Johannesburg with her new husband.

While I sat in her book-lined office, she completely changed the picture for me with her announcement: 'The recently appointed professor is going to introduce a course-work master's degree. He'll teach international law of the sea but he wants someone to teach a new course on the South African coastal area – coastal zone law.' It immediately hit me that coastal zone law was in effect environmental law of the indeterminate coastal area comprising both land and sea.

I sprang into action and immediately applied for the job, even though the closing date was still a month away. But at the same time I also wondered whether my newly discovered HIV status, about which I kept mum, might somehow disqualify me.

Sometime later, I heard that I was shortlisted and that I'd be interviewed in due course. I waited anxiously. Then, on the appointed day, I nervously entered the interview room and found the selection committee – all white men in those days – seated in a half-moon circle around me. The newly appointed professor chaired the interview and asked a number of easy practical questions such as, 'Would you be prepared to teach coastal zone law?' Would I? Of course, I would! I wanted to shout, but instead I politely answered yes. Afterwards I thought I'd not shown enough enthusiasm to get the job. A week or so later, my friend and colleague Dennis Davis passed me in the quadrangle and impishly announced, 'You're coming second!' Second, of course, was as good as last.

But I did get a letter in the post offering me the job. Alarmingly, it was accompanied by a form that had to be completed by a medical doctor certifying that I was in good health. I spent another few sleepless nights before going to the local doctor on Main Road. I disclosed my HIV status, but he simply shrugged his shoulders, saying, 'I'm sure it will be fine,' and signed the form.

Encouraged by Liz, I went to a psychologist for the first time, paranoid that my HIV-positive status would become public. From those early sessions, I learned two important things: I must deal with my feelings of anger (which I struggle with to this day); and, despite my HIV-positive status, women were likely to be amenable to a relationship (which turned out to be correct).

*

After accepting the new position, I immediately set about preparing lecture notes to teach coastal zone law in the next academic year, in addition to completing my environmental mini-dissertation. My challenge was that coastal law was not a regular legal discipline taught anywhere in South Africa, nor were there textbooks on the subject from which I could draw, apart from one American book on coastal law in the law library. As the internet had not been heard of in those days, I drew on journal articles and consulted natural science colleagues who enthusiastically assisted me in identifying environmental problems that required a legal lens. In this way, I managed to cobble together a cohesive set of lecture notes for my initial teaching. These stood me in good stead not only when I introduced environmental law as an optional course in the final LLB, and then at master's level, but especially later when I embarked on writing the book *Environmental Law in South Africa*, first published in 2000, a milestone year which I had sometimes wondered whether I would live to see. The book has remained my academic foundation stone. It is now published in loose-leaf format and is updated annually. All the while I kept quiet about my life-threatening disease: this knowledge drove me and kept me focused on my budding academic career.

While undertaking this early research I would come across foreign law journals containing articles on the link between human rights law and environmental law as well as constitutional law. I put these refences aside in what I then called my 'dream file', thinking that, one day, maybe, in the very far future apartheid might fall and these references could be valuable. Little did I know that these would prove vital much sooner than I thought.

In 1989, the year before the termination of South Africa's unlawful occupation of the territory then known as South West Africa, I received a phone call from Professor Fuggle in the now renamed Department of Environmental and Geographical Sciences. 'There is a chap on the line from Windhoek who says they need help with drafting an environmental right for the future Namibian constitution,' he said. Then he transferred the call to me.

An official in the South West African Department of Nature Conservation was at the other end of the line. I would later meet the red-bearded Chris Brown, but at the time I said that I would be happy to assist, asking, 'How many months do I have?'

'Three weeks,' he responded.

Fortunately, I had my 'dream file' on hand. I submitted a memorandum providing motivation for an environmental right in the future Namibian constitution, drawing on international writings on developments in the area of human and environmental rights, which I had been collecting. Chris tweaked the document and steered it through the correct political channels. In the end, the Namibian constitution did not include a classical environmental right, though it did include a directive on state policy that referred to the environment. It was the first country in Africa to do so. I couldn't help wondering if the spirit of those Namib desert beetles in my friend Guy's empty fish tank had anything to do with this.

*

In February 1990 Namibia adopted a new democratic constitution and became officially independent in March. February 1990 also saw FW de Klerk making his landmark speech at the opening of Parliament, announcing the unbanning of the ANC and the release of political prisoners, including Nelson Mandela, in addition to other sweeping reforms. I realised that South Africa would in all probability move in the same direction as Namibia and adopt a new constitutional order. I set about immersing all my research efforts in the study of the somewhat uncharted concept of the right to a decent environment in a country's constitution. Others around me were canvassing for less vague rights such as the right to education, medical care, housing, and so on. All of these fell into the category of 'socio-economic rights' and were not considered by conventional legal scholars to be appropriate for inclusion in a constitution. This is because they imply a positive duty on the part of the state to provide such rights, in contrast to classical 'civil and political' rights, such as the right to vote or freedom of expression, which merely require the state to desist from interfering in a citizen's right to vote or to express a view.

Talk of a new constitution and a bill of rights for the new South Africa was in the air. As a result of my Namibian input, and out of the blue, through the intervention of some Stellenbosch Law Faculty colleagues, I was invited by the Commonwealth Law Association to a conference on constitution making and environmental rights. The political situation in South Africa was ripe for the topic.

It was with great excitement and some trepidation that I took the eleven-hour trip to London at this time to present a ten-minute paper on constitutional environmental rights, at a time when the environment did not generally feature in national constitutions. I was an unconfident junior academic, sometimes even feeling like an impostor but keen to make my mark. I had with me drafts of both the South African government's and the ANC's proposed environmental clauses. The latter had apparently been drafted by Albie Sachs and Kader Asmal on a kitchen table while they were still in exile. I was pleased that my presentation on a possible environmental right in a future bill of rights was enthusiastically received.

At that time, I 'adopted' as a mentor the indomitable Denis Cowen, an octogenarian legal scholar who was reputedly the brains behind the defence in resisting the removal of coloured people from the common voters' roll in the 1950s. I would visit him on many a Cape winter's evening in his cosy Mowbray home where he once declared, sitting next to his fireplace, whisky in hand, 'All law is environmental law,' as he beckoned his wife to bring 'some more of that delicious cheese and olives'.

Environmental law was not a recognised discipline at the time in South Africa. Instead – in the words of Professor André Rabie, who'd come weekly from Stellenbosch University to teach us during my environmental master's degree – the subject was a collection of principles from different branches of the law, such as criminal law and administrative law. The crucial point to emerge from my fireside chats with Denis Cowen was that if environmental law was to be recognised as a subject, it had to develop distinctive principles. Indeed, Cowen went on to publish a seminal article titled 'Environmental Law: A Subject Struggling to Be Born'.

While I regard Cowen as the father of environmental law in South Africa, whether consciously or subconsciously I took on the role of midwife, hoping to deliver the baby. The time was right. South Africa was embarking on negotiating a new constitution, including a bill of rights. I set about researching the rather ethereal notion of 'the right to a decent environment' – a topic easy to talk about in everyday conversation, but the question was whether the notion could be embedded in law. I found some leads and inspiration from the Indian jurisprudence, thanks to Advocate Geoff Budlender, who pointed me in that direction.

It was on one of my London visits that I made contact with and befriended Richard Macrory, a leading British environmental law academic and counsel based then at University College London. We connected immediately, and it was he who, on one of these visits, suggested walking down the corridor to meet his colleague Philippe Sands, who had then just published a leading textbook, *International Environmental Law*, more or less at the same time that I launched my own *Environmental Law in South Africa*. Little was I to know then that I would meet Philippe decades later, for very different reasons, in Lviv.

Very soon after the unbanning of the ANC, I was thrilled to be invited to a closed conference, at Maccauvlei on the banks of the Vaal River, focusing on environmental rights. I was overawed by the attendees, who were legal and political luminaries on both sides of the political divide. The conference paper delivered by Albie Sachs, titled 'You Don't Have to Be White to Be Green', was, I believe, his first to be delivered locally after his return from exile. While Sachs was presenting his paper, I sat nervously in the small lecture room, for the umpteenth time going over my paper motivating for environmental rights in a new constitutional dispensation. I was to present it straight after him. In front of me was seated Justice Pierre Olivier, who chaired the committee that had recently produced the South African Law Commission's draft report on protecting minority rights. While Sachs was presenting his talk, I took a deep breath, tapped the judge on the shoulder, and handed him a copy of my paper. He paged through it and, after a few minutes, mumbled under his breath, 'Jislaaik, this is fantastic.' I had made my mark.

For me, the realisation that I was witnessing a key moment in South Africa's political transformation came when, at the end of that day's formal session, I witnessed Pierre Olivier, with my paper in hand, summon Albie Sachs to a back room, saying, 'Kom, laat ons praat' (Come, let's talk). That was a watershed moment for my budding environmental law career.

An environmental right was eventually included in the bill of rights chapter of the South African Constitution, and it was almost a decade later that the first significant judicial statement on the environmental right was made by the very same judge, Pierre Olivier, who stated in the Supreme Court of Appeal: 'Our Constitution, by including environmental rights as fundamental justiciable human rights, by necessary implication requires that environmental considerations be accorded appropriate recognition and respect in the administrative process in our country.'

This was the culmination of the most exciting time of my thirty-year academic career.

*

In the year after John Major became UK prime minister in November 1990, I visited a friend from my UCT law school days. He was then living in Sussex and practising law. As I stepped off the train at Waterloo Station on my return journey, a newspaper vendor dropped a pile of the *Evening Standard* at my feet. I glanced down, and my eye fell on a front-page headline: 'Major Agrees to Compensation for Infected Blood Transfusions'. I started reading the article while still fumbling for my wallet. The gist of it was that Parliament had agreed to compensate British haemophiliacs who had contracted the HI virus from contaminated blood products, or their families in the case of those who had died. I was excited but initially angry, as I am not British. But it soon dawned on me that I had spent over a year in the UK as an LLM student at the LSE and had regularly visited the Haemophilia Centre at the Royal Free Hospital. I have vivid memories of catching the Northern Line and disembarking at Belsize Park. It must have been during this time that I contracted the virus. I read the article over and over, but there was no indication of how to apply for compensation. I did not pursue the issue at the time, and flew back to Cape Town.

Some months afterwards, another UCT friend who was also practising law in the UK let me know that he was visiting Cape Town and invited me for a Sunday excursion up the West Coast to see the annual wild flowers. We were accompanied by his friends, also from the UK, one of whom was Gigi, who caught my eye. Pretty and blonde, she was a lawyer whose work had something to do with the Cheshire Homes charity trust. On the drive I learned that she specialised in medico-legal law in London. I disclosed to her that I was HIV-positive, and told her about the UK compensation award. She listened with keen interest, and suggested that I send her the details about my treatment at the Royal Free Hospital. I did so, and then forgot all about it.

Sometime later, I returned from UCT after a tiring day, and, as usual, my first task after feeding my two cats was to empty the letter-box of its usual pile of advertising flyers and bills. But this time there was a crisp official-looking envelope. I opened it and found a cheque for £20 000, along with a covering letter from Gigi's law firm.

I was so taken aback that I ran around the perimeter of my house in excitement.

The envelope included a one-page form for me to complete, stating where and when I had received blood products in the UK and any other medically acquired conditions. I learned that the British government, through the agency of Gigi's law firm, had added me without further inquiry to the cohort of British haemophiliacs who were being compensated for having received contaminated blood. This included not only people like me who had acquired HIV, but also those who'd contracted hepatitis B and C. The lump sum was followed by a monthly *ex gratia* payment, which I squirrelled away in a UK bank account for a rainy day.

In addition, a Los Angeles law firm ran a worldwide class action on a contingency fee basis (no success, no legal fees payable) on behalf of non-US haemophiliacs who had received infected blood products. They recruited me as their South African man on the ground. I felt as if I were part of an American TV movie set when I met their representatives at a five-star Waterfront hotel in Cape Town and later was flown to an equivalent hotel in Johannesburg, where we had to search for treatment records at the Johannesburg General Hospital. This also ended in my receiving financial compensation.

The rainy day never came, so years later I used the funds from both these sources to buy a run-down pre-war flat in Cracow, which Gabriel, my cousin Ewa's husband, and my wife, Louise, an architect, helped renovate. Apart from the pleasure of having a flat in a historic city in Europe, it served me as a perfect launch pad for my later escapades into Ukraine. Later it was to give me great satisfaction to make it available to Ukrainian refugees fleeing the Russian invasion.

In addition to enabling me to purchase the flat, the monthly compensation payments continue to the present day, ensuring that I have a healthy supplement to my UCT pension. For this I am grateful.

*

A few years after starting my career at UCT, and after working with intensity and much gusto, I had a sudden urge to get away from computers and books and do something different for a while. I felt a need to work with my hands and considered doing a gardening or woodwork course. But then a postgraduate student I knew suggested a pottery course in the village of McGregor, some two hours' drive from Cape Town, which I had heard about but never visited. She told me about the Banks family, Jane and Ian, who ran week-long residential pottery courses from their home. Perfect, right up my street, I thought. I phoned Jane and booked to attend the next course, which was only scheduled to take place early the following year.

Subsequently I heard that Jane and Ian's son Wally, an HIV-positive gay man, had tragically taken his own life on Chapman's Peak. His death had been reported on the front page of the *Cape Times*. He was unable to share his HIV burden with anybody, not even with his parents, who were unaware that he was gay: such was the shame in the 1990s. At the time, the AIDS epidemic was just appearing in South Africa and was casting a dark shadow over many people's lives, though it was only spoken about in whispers.

I had not yet met Jane in person, but I phoned to offer my condolences and to find out about the forthcoming course, which I expected would be cancelled. 'No,' she said. 'We have decided to continue. There will be some friends of Wally on the course.' So, a few weeks later I made my first trip to McGregor. I arrived in the evening and was met by Ian at the gate. His first words to me were 'Oppas vir die bekklapper' in a jocular reference to the farm-gate lock.

The pottery course was wonderful. I loved the squishy clay, the feeling of getting my hands dirty, the chatter in the studio among my newly acquainted fellow students. Jane was always there to offer a helping hand – and, as she would later tell me, to see what she could glean about each person's character from the way they worked the clay.

I thought about disclosing my own HIV status to Jane even though I had known her for less than a week. And yet I had this inexplicable urge to divulge my status to her, to share my big secret, my 'shameful' burden. She would in all likelihood be angry, I thought. Her son had recently taken his own life, but I was still alive.

One late afternoon I saw her silhouetted against the sunset, watering her beloved garden. Our group class for the day had finished. I took a deep breath and approached her.

'Jane, there's something I need to tell you,' I blurted. 'I'm also HIV-positive.'

This was a turning point. She immediately hugged me, and in the coming years she would embrace me emotionally too. For the next five or six decades she was to become a soulmate, a mother figure, a confidante and an adviser. With her husband, Jane provided a refuge in the sleepy village of McGregor – away from my busy academic life in lonely Cape Town. More than once she said to me, 'Mi casa es su casa' (my house is your house). We shared many fun evenings in their sprawling double-storey house, often listening to music, as Ian played the flute.

I became a regular visitor to the Bankses in McGregor, my home from home.

*

It was during this period that I would, when time allowed, visit my half-sister Adela, the youngest of the rugby scrum of fourteen children, and her husband, Brett. They enjoy an earthy lifestyle in Rheenendal, near Knysna; their flourishing smallholding literally abuts the verdant Knysna Forest. They grow food, Adela creates painted T-shirts for the Sedgefield market, and Brett surfs at nearby Buffalo (Buffels) Bay whenever he gets the chance.

I followed with keen interest the home birth of their youngest daughter, Layla, in 1995. She is the youngest of the over thirty grandchildren of my parents, given the combined 'yours-ours-and-my' nature of our family. After her birth I was fascinated to hear from Adela that she felt very strongly the presence of our late father in the room while she was giving birth to Layla at home. I took a keen interest in Layla's growing-up years and observed her as she went from one interest to another; equally fascinated by human behaviour and by the natural world, she seemed a good candidate for a natural science degree. Her free spirit and her search for more practical learning resulted in her sensibly ignoring my advice to study further at UCT or Stellenbosch. Instead she embarked on a study of life by going abroad for five years straight after matriculating. Here she worked hard to fund her own travels, learning by doing, working in hospitality across Europe and then following the footsteps of her grandfather and becoming more and more passionate about food systems and farming. I would receive emails from her addressed to 'Dear Nutty Uncle' as she assisted on farms in New Zealand, Australia and India, while I would in turn respond to her as my 'Dear Nomad Niece'.

CHAPTER 7

Living and Working with HIV

IN THE mid-1990s, I was contacted again by Chris Brown, who had been instrumental in my involvement in drafting an environmental clause for the Namibian constitution some five years previously. He had, in the interim, become head of the Namibian Directorate of Environmental Affairs. I eagerly accepted his invitation to spend a year in his department, assisting with the revision of the newly independent state's environmental laws. I was fortunate to secure unpaid leave from UCT to do this exciting work, and to have the university's assurance I could return to my post upon completion of the Namibian project.

I set off in my newly acquired white Ford Bantam bakkie to make the two-day journey to Windhoek up the N7, crossing the border at the Vioolsdrif post. It was late afternoon; the sun was setting and casting red-gold shimmers over the open plain. I marvelled at how few vehicles there were on the national highway, perhaps two or three every hour, and unleashed Van Morrison at full blast to the wide world outside. I reflected on how my love of and connection to the wide-open spaces of Namibia had first been instilled when my stepbrothers John and Martin and I spent a winter holiday in Ovamboland as schoolboys. Later, during my environmental studies years, I visited a university pal, Clinton, who was working there as an exploration geologist. It turned out to be an unusual occasion as we and his staff had to be up at dawn to peg a claim to prevent the possibility of a rival mining company muscling in. I felt as if I was back in the old gold rush days.

Initially I lived on a smallholding some 15 kilometres outside Windhoek. It was lonely there, so I moved to a farm cottage on the outskirts of the suburb of Avis, where my morning commute to work would on occasion be interrupted by kudu crossing the dirt road as I set off. My work necessitated that I drive sometimes to outlying areas of the country to consult with game rangers and others. On one occasion I travelled with a legal colleague to the Epupa Falls on the Kunene River to confer with the local Himba chief about a controversial proposed hydroelectric dam-building project. It was on one of these trips to the far north of the country that my HIV-positive friend, Caddie Khadeboux, came to visit from England and accompanied me. He was rather alarmed when I informed him that we were returning with a live but deadly zebra cobra in the back of the bakkie for a snake collector in Windhoek.

Although I had a fulfilling job in Namibia, I felt lonely and the old cloud of depression started settling in. At the same time, my energy levels seemed depleted. I was not taking antiretroviral drugs as these were not generally available at the time. And I was not yet familiar with the notion of viral load, which measures the amount of HI virus in a person, nor did I know about the CD4-count marker – which is a measure of one's immunity. A normal healthy person has a CD4 count of over 600, and HIV-positive people were considered to have full-blown AIDS if their CD4 count dropped to below 200. My condition got progressively worse, and after a year I felt on the edge of a mental breakdown. With the encouragement of my work colleagues, I decided to leave Namibia, and flew back to Cape Town where there were better medical facilities. My other favourite niece, Michaela, and her husband flew to Windhoek to fetch my Ford bakkie, pack up my possessions and bring them back to Cape Town.

I returned to my post at UCT but initially had difficulty gathering my thoughts to start teaching again. I was not well, and was referred to a GP who specialised in HIV treatment. He discovered that my viral load was in the millions and my CD4 count was teetering on the 200 mark. He recommended front-line HIV drugs, which I had to take three times a day. They made me feel absolutely awful: nauseous and light-headed. I started skipping doses and adopted the attitude that what must be must be. Moreover, my thighs, which were never very bulky, became exceedingly thin – so much so that today they are still like matchsticks. An associated side effect of the medication was body fat redistribution: while my limbs and bottom became thin, my paunch became larger. A friend jokingly ascribed this to the good life.

As I had to teach when I got back to UCT, I needed to pull myself together, and I regained my old mental self fairly quickly. Shortly after my return, and on the advice of doctors at the Western Cape Blood Service, which was responsible for issuing my factor VIII, I approached Dr Gordon Isaacs, a counsellor closely associated with the Gay Association of South Africa (GASA). AIDS was still a new phenomenon in the late 1990s, and there was, as yet, no available counselling facility. Thus it was that I found myself standing early one summer evening under the shadow of Table Mountain, at GASA's offices near the top of Bree Street.

I was feeling somewhat uneasy as I painfully climbed the half-dozen steps. If one of my students saw me there, would they think I was gay? Would heads turn as I walked in? Would someone hit on me? But no one seemed to notice my entrance, and my presence appeared not to attract any attention at all.

I thought back on the time when I was an articled clerk in a Johannesburg law firm. Gayness was then not really spoken about. I'd befriended a very dear work colleague, Trevor, who'd invited me to dinner at his flat, and I remember him clasping my hands and telling me how beautiful they were. I was not keen on anything other than a platonic relationship and encouraged him to find 'a nice Italian boy' – this was shortly before his departure to that country. He did just that, and my advice may have helped him accept his sexual preference. We remain firm friends to this day. Many years later, at my wedding, he hugged me and told me how happy he was for me that I had found a special person to share my life with.

It was difficult being HIV-positive but not gay. It somehow exacerbated my loneliness.

*

At this stage of my life, my joints, particularly the hinge joints (ankles, knees and elbows), as opposed to ball-and-socket joints (hips), had become severely damaged and increasingly painful. This was a consequence of countless episodes of haemophilia-induced internal bleeding into the joint space, resulting in osteoarthritis. The initial cause was kicking soccer balls as a kid, walking down steep mountainsides, and so on. My knees were the first parts of my body that needed attention, but I could not decide whether to replace the left or the right one first. I arranged an exploratory consultation with a specialist knee surgeon, Dr G.

It was summer then and occasionally I would take my boisterous Border collie named Oscar Wild (*sic*) for a walk. One late afternoon, I took him to Camps Bay beach after leaving work early. As I alighted from my car with Oscar on a leash, I noticed an attractive woman in a cheesecloth skirt nearby. We smiled at each other. I set off in the opposite direction, kicking myself for not having started a conversation: I would have little chance of seeing her again on the crowded summer beach. But then, as I returned to my car, there she was, looking at me in some distress. It turned out that she had lost her car keys and wondered if I could give her a lift back to Rondebosch to collect her spare set.

'Absolutely, no problem at all,' I replied, at the same time thanking my guardian angels for setting up this encounter. As we approached

Kloof Nek, I was telling her about my imminent knee replacement surgery. She announced that her fiancé was the eminent surgeon Dr G.

I scheduled the surgery for late January 1996.

*

Shortly before my knee replacement surgery, England were playing South Africa in the traditional New Year's cricket match at Newlands. I was glued to the TV as 'Gogga' Adams, a left-arm spin bowler with an unconventional, ungainly action, had come in to bat. South Africa were in trouble, not having enough runs on the board. Adams hit a four, and the crowd was immediately ecstatic.

I wanted to watch more, but I had to take Paul E to the airport. He had been staying with me for the past five years or so, having moved down from Johannesburg to work in Cape Town. I had known him since we first connected through the South African Haemophilia Foundation, while I'd been working in Johannesburg. Not only were we both haemophiliacs, but we were also both HIV-positive. We used to compare notes over supper about common issues including various alternative remedies that were touted at the time. We'd both managed to get on a trial at Tygerberg Hospital for an immune-boosting drug that eventually became marketed under the brand name Moducare.

Paul had not been well for the past year, unable to eat, and suffering terrible diarrhoea. He'd visibly deteriorated after a trip to Europe, with an overnight stop in Cairo, where he suspected he picked up the Giardia parasite. That apparently was what was causing his stomach problems. He had always been lean, but he was getting thinner and more gaunt. He'd spent the previous few weeks packing up his rooms and sorting out his affairs. He'd also taken the trouble to return the vegetarian *Moosewood Cookbook*, which he'd borrowed from Liz months before, and which had been lying since then in the kitchen drawer.

Just as I was about to get up and leave for the airport, Adams hit another four. Neither Paul nor I wanted to get up, or say goodbye. But we had to go. Paul swung his rucksack into the boot and I tuned into the cricket commentary on my car radio. I didn't much listen to what Paul was saying on the highway, as Adams had now gone out. Paul had been talking about the fact that he had not paid rent that month, but I muttered, 'Don't worry – pay when you get back.' I added something inane about having a dinner party when he returned. I decided not to turn into the airport parking lot, as England were now coming in to bat. I would just drop him at the entrance to the departure area. Paul was ten years younger than me. The specialist HIV/AIDS physician Dr Gary Maartens claims there is statistical evidence that HIV-positive people are more likely to die at my age than at Paul's.

But Paul never did come back. After my knee replacement at Wynberg Southern Cross Hospital, when the medical team had established that all had gone well, they told me Paul had died in Johannesburg General Hospital. I was supposed to have died before him.

*

Whenever I was in the UK, I always used to visit Caddie Khadeboux in his terrace house in Brighton. After the death of his wife, Debbie, he talked mostly with the two Persian cats who lived with him; he also meditated regularly. He was the person nearest to a practising Buddhist I have ever known. We exchanged notes and yarns about blood products in the UK and South Africa, about living with HIV, and about women, including an ex-girlfriend who was Polish – I would pump him for information about her – and Debbie, whom he had loved very much. He had visited me in Namibia shortly before we shared that historic Saturday in 1995 when South Africa, against all odds, beat the All Blacks at the Rugby World Cup final at Ellis Park. We had driven to Cardiff that morning to watch the match with Gary, yet another HIV-positive haemophiliac, who was a Welsh rugby fanatic, and together we watched Madiba famously don the number 6 Springbok jersey. In cold Cardiff I did not sense any of the euphoria that gripped my country when Joel Stransky kicked the winning drop goal.

On one of these visits to Brighton, for some inexplicable reason, I spontaneously asked Caddie, 'Who do I phone if I can't get hold of you?' We were standing on the platform at Brighton station and I was about to return to London. The grimy neon sign read: 'Next train Waterloo: 2 minutes'. I hugged him as the train approached, grabbed my overnight bag, and boarded the train.

But now, I was talking through the open train window when Caddie hastily said, 'Amina, my sister in London, here's her number.' I jotted it down on a scrap of paper. 'Keep well,' we said in unison as we waved each other goodbye.

Two years later, I was in London again. I arrived in the early hours, having been on the overnight flight from Cape Town. This time I was en route to Malmö in Sweden, where I was due to give a paper at a conference. I arrived on a Monday morning and phoned Caddie almost immediately after settling into my niece's flat. There was no reply, just his soft melodious voice on the answering machine, so I left a message for him to call me back.

Later in the afternoon I tried Caddie again. And again I got an answering machine. Maybe he was away for a few days. Then I remembered that, despite my hasty packing, I had brought my phone book, and congratulated myself for having transcribed Amina's number. So I phoned her. A young girl answered, telling me, 'Mom's still at work.' I explained I was Caddie's friend from South Africa, and could her mother please phone me back.

An hour later I received a call. 'Caddie is definitely around, I talked to him just this Sunday,' said Amina. 'I have heard much about you. Caddie spoke with much fondness about you and his visit to Namibia when you were working there. It would be nice to meet you. He said he was feeling tired but well. He's probably just out for the day. Keep trying.'

I tried again on Tuesday and Wednesday, without any luck. I phoned Amina on Wednesday evening. She'd had a tiring day at work and said she would get back to me. And she did, the next day. She echoed my worry and suggested that she drive down to Brighton, but she would have to get off work.

'Would you like me to come with you?' I offered.

'That would be lovely. We can take the scenic route,' she said.

On the drive down to Brighton I felt more and more uneasy. But Amina chatted amiably about her views on South Africa, about Caddie, and her family. As we turned into his street she cheerfully exclaimed: 'There's his car – he's there!' She double-parked and I went to the door. When I knocked, I noticed that the milk had not been collected. I heard a cat's melancholy meowing. I stood waiting, then went back to the car. Amina said, 'He's probably taken his cats to the vet by taxi so he wouldn't have to drive.' But I sensed that this was not the case. Then Amina had an idea: the neighbour had a key. But she was not back from work. So we went to have a sandwich at a local bistro and left a note for the neighbour to call us when she returned, which she duly did.

Back to the house. Now we had a key. I thought: Amina is family, she must enter first. I opened the door and let her pass into the house. First the lounge, then the kitchen. No sound except for a mournful meowing. Up the stairs, Amina first. On the landing we peered into the spare room. This was where I'd slept the last time I stayed there. Ascending the last flight, Amina rushed up to his bedroom. 'He's been here!' she cried triumphantly. 'His bed is not made.' I was still on the landing, where the bathroom was. The door was ever so slightly open. I pushed at it but it wouldn't move. I then tried again. When it still wouldn't give, I realised Caddie's body was lying sprawled across the bathroom floor. I put my hand though the opening and touched his shoulder. He was ice cold, but he looked peaceful. I glanced at the hand basin. It was half filled with water, and his shaving gear was neatly set out.

'Amina!' I gasped, 'it's the worst.'

'Oh no,' she wailed.

'Do you want to see him?'

'No,' she cried.

'What should I do?'

'Phone 111,' she sobbed.

The medical service arrived within minutes, then the ambulance, followed by the police. I was staggered at the efficiency and impressed by how empathetic they all were. The policewoman questioned me while her colleague was upstairs. It dawned on me that I was being interrogated about this 'sudden death', and I explained my link to Caddie, the fact that we were both HIV-positive haemophiliacs, and that I'd been spending a few days in London en route to Sweden to attend a conference.

Caddie's personal doctor arrived soon afterwards. Amina asked me whether I wanted any of her brother's belongings. 'His walking stick,' I said. He had offered to buy me one when we were returning from Cardiff, but I had declined. I tentatively asked his doctor what would happen to his factor VIII in his fridge: it was far more concentrated than the South African product and therefore less bulky to travel with. I was happy when the doctor told me I could have it. On Caddie's death we became blood brothers.

The next day was 11 November, Armistice Day, and friends in Cambridge had arranged for me to attend an evening performance of John Rutter's *Requiem*. As I sat in King's College Chapel, the enchanting sounds reverberated around me, and midway through the performance, the floodgates opened, and I wept and wept.

I would later learn that Caddie died of pneumocystis pneumonia, a common cause of death among HIV-positive people.

That was in the late 1990s, and I wondered whether I would make the millennium or suffer the same fate as Caddie. I resolved to soldier on. In 1999 I bought a quarter-share in a beach cottage at Rooi-Els on False Bay for a song. It was there that I enjoyed the company of friends as we saw in the new millennium. After careful deliberation, the first piece of music I played the next morning to mark the start of that auspicious year was John Lennon's 'Imagine'.

*

The year 2000 saw Durban host the 13th International AIDS Conference. Coincidentally, the annual South African Law Teachers' Conference was being held in Durban at the same time. I had attended previous conferences, but now had the option of going instead to the AIDS meeting, where delegates included scientists, clinicians, health-care workers, public health agencies and people living with HIV/AIDS. I was tempted to attend, but I was once again in a dark period, feeling depressed. The thought of entering an alien environment filled with thousands of delegates, and not knowing a single person, did not appeal. And so I attended the Law Teachers' Conference instead.

Afterwards I read in the press that at the opening event of the AIDS conference, Nkosi Johnson, who was 11 years old at the time, addressed the assembly and gave a moving account of how he was born HIV-positive, and sought acceptance of his condition. I was aware of reports that he had been discriminated against at his Johannesburg school. Nkosi died the following year. I could fully identify with him when his adoptive mother disclosed that she had found his antiretroviral pills under his bed. He could not stand taking them. I well understood why: the side effects were very unpleasant.

At the same conference, Edwin Cameron, an eminent South African lawyer and later a justice of the Constitutional Court, gave an impassioned speech about living with HIV, stating that he was alive only because he was able to afford antiretroviral drugs, while tens of thousands of South Africans could not. I drew great comfort from the fact that he publicly disclosed his status and gained confidence as a result. Edwin became a role model for me.

*

As I have mentioned, my relationship with antiretroviral drugs was an unhappy one because of the side effects. By a fortunate coincidence, I was invited by the warden of Smuts Hall (now Upper Campus Residence), a colleague, to a dinner function one evening. I found myself seated next to a senior academic, Professor Peter Folb, then head of the Department of Pharmacology. By the time we progressed to the dessert, I'd gathered up my courage and proceeded to tell him of my HIV status. He seemed rather shocked, and recommended that I see Dr Catherine Orrell, who was with the Desmond Tutu HIV Centre at Groote Schuur Hospital, and who was involved in clinical trials and the roll-out of HIV drugs in the townships. Upon meeting Catherine, I was immediately taken by her gentle yet no-nonsense attitude.

I was anxious and depressed about my blood markers, and reluctant to continue the first-line drugs I was half-heartedly taking, as they made me feel nauseous and light-headed. Catherine looked at me hard, and then drew a sketch of a train approaching a cliff. 'The speed of the train is your HIV viral load,' she said. 'The distance from the cliff is your CD4 count.' This depiction hit me like a thunderbolt.

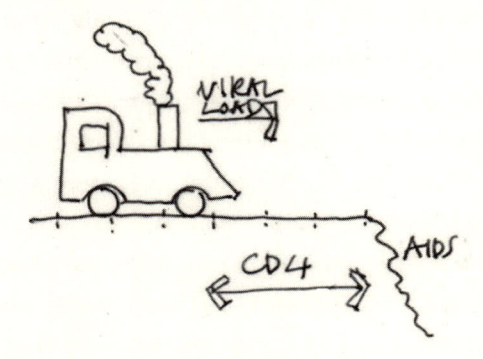

The problem, as I understood it, was that up till then I had been dabbling with the first-line HIV drugs that were available on the market. The accepted view at the time was that if one had not been taking these first-line drugs properly, one would have built up a resistance, so there was no point in taking any other standard drugs such as AZT. The analogy was that of a chess game. The pawns were the standard drugs, which I had by-passed, and now I was playing with my knights, bishop and queen. For a while, my cocktail had included nevirapine, which is known to cause people to have vivid dreams. In my case the 'vivid dreams' became hallucinatory, adding to my discomfort in taking the cocktail. But Catherine encouraged me by telling me that a Rastafarian patient of hers had stopped taking marijuana as he found the nevirapine-containing cocktail a good substitute.

Catherine went on to explain the various medical categories of drugs, which I struggled to get my head around: nucleoside reverse transcriptase inhibitors (NRTIs), which prevent HIV from replicating by blocking an enzyme called reverse transcriptase; and non-nucleoside reverse transcriptase inhibitors (NNRTIs), which prevent HIV from replicating by binding to and altering reverse transcriptase, which HIV uses to reproduce. Both categories reduce one's viral load. Apart from becoming familiar with names such as abacavir, efavirenz, lamivudine, nevirapine, tenofovir and many other medications, I also had to learn about their various side effects. To add to the complexity, if two drugs are combined into one pill, they have a different brand name.

Even though I had been put on these front-line drugs and had, as it were, used up my pawns, Catherine suggested I try to revert to this, the older, standard regime. She put me on a triple combination of AZT and 3TC with efavirenz. 'Let's see what happens,' she said with a reassuring smile.

I had my levels checked again a month or so later, and when Catherine reported back on my blood tests, I was overjoyed to hear that my viral load had dropped dramatically and that my CD4 count had vastly improved. Catherine had managed not only to slow the train down but also to push it back from the edge of the cliff.

*

It was a Tuesday morning, and I was back in full swing at UCT, teaching marine and environmental law. Among the clutter of emails that confronted me as I arrived rather late at my office was a notification of an urgent meeting of the medical ethics group. The topic to be discussed was a needle-stick injury. A Groote Schuur Hospital surgeon had performed an emergency operation on a trauma patient the previous Friday night. The patient had been in a severe car accident, and so the surgeon amputated the leg that had been crushed. While performing the operation, he had inadvertently stuck a needle into himself. Two or three days later, the patient's HIV test came back – it was HIV-positive. This was the mid-1990s, and no protocol had as yet been developed for dealing with this situation. The issues to be discussed by the medical ethics group were: What should the hospital do in this particular instance? What was its long-term policy with regard to needle-stick injuries?

A colleague and friend in the Law Faculty had nominated me for this multidisciplinary discussion group. Although it largely comprised Groote Schuur Hospital doctors and other medical staff, there were also philosophers and social scientists. I would be representing the legal side. My colleague, the late Ina Ackermann, had exuberantly told me that I would be replacing her on the group, and that I would enjoy this wonderful and interesting group, convened by the dynamic Professor Solly Benatar. It generally met once a month to discuss a variety of complex ethical issues surrounding medical practice in the context of the newly transformed, democratic South Africa. Among the difficult and fascinating topics considered by the committee were euthanasia, organ donation and the provision of medical care to prisoners.

I was well suited to the group, not so much because of my legal background but because of my insider's view of how hospitals worked, based on my experience ever since early childhood. The very wards I walked past on my way to these meetings were those where I had often been a patient, and where an earlier cohort of professors would discuss my condition in their daily ward rounds. Now, I would be seeing the hospital from the other side.

Apart from a few exceptions, I had, at the time, disclosed my HIV status to very few people. On one particular day, the usual austere meeting room was not available, and so instead we met on an enclosed balcony high up, overlooking the Observatory Main Road. I felt a slight headache in the left part of my forehead as the white-coated doctors and other colleagues pulled up their chairs in a horseshoe. I noticed a few familiar faces: Solly Benatar, the head of Surgery, the head of Cardiology, and a few new faces too. The big guns were all there for the meeting.

The discussion centred on whether Surgeon X should be treated immediately with AZT. Someone pointed out that, according to the literature, only a small fraction of needle-stick injuries from HIV/AIDS patients go on to develop HIV. The debate moved on to related topics: the need for all staff to wear gloves; whether treatment should be postponed in order to check the HIV status of patients; and the problem of how to deal with emergencies. I found myself lost in a reverie about the fact that AZT was never made available to haemophiliacs who were infected with HIV from blood products supplied by the hospital. That question was never even debated.

The white-coated doctor next to me seemed particularly animated, cutting into my thoughts.

'It's no longer a disease up in Africa. It's only a problem down there,' he said, gesturing towards Observatory and the Cape Flats beyond.

I had an urge to tap him on the shoulder and whisper into his ear: 'It's actually sitting right next to you, old chap…'

But I said nothing. The meeting closed with the decision to treat the surgeon immediately with AZT. I walked wearily down the corridor, and caught the lift down to the ground floor. As I came out into the summer glare, I felt my head pounding. I had a blinding headache.

At the beginning of the next academic year Solly Benatar asked all the members of the group to review their contributions to the committee. I then told them about my HIV status. It was quite a relief. My headaches seemed to subside after that. I'm grateful that I was introduced to this vibrant group.

*

Some years later I had my left ankle fused. By that time it had become painful to walk to the bathroom in the morning. Before the surgery, I disclosed my HIV status to the surgeon at Claremont Hospital, and was dumbfounded when he said, 'In that case I can't operate.'

'Use gloves,' I suggested. This was in any case already the protocol at the time.

'It's not me I'm worried about; it's my operating staff,' he responded.

By coincidence, Krysia's friend Colleen, who was also a friend of mine, was a theatre sister in the same ward. I had discussed the pros and cons of my intended operation with her, and we'd joked about the possibility of her being on duty that day.

'Colleen M— is a friend, and would be happy to assist,' I told the surgeon.

The operation went ahead.

*

I feel slightly uneasy, a tension in the pit of my stomach. It is a coolish early spring day in late September. It is that in-between time in the academic year when lectures are winding down but the final exam period has not begun. I had spoken the previous week about being diagnosed with HIV to a group of university staff. I think it is for this reason that I have now been invited by Dr Wendy Orr, head of Student

Health at UCT, to give a talk to student wardens from various universities and a few other members of the UCT community.

I have prepared a few notes, and it strikes me that this is the first time that I'll be giving a public talk on living with HIV. I am now combining my formal academic activities with the turmoil in my personal life. The knot in my stomach tightens as Dr Orr introduces me, even though the atmosphere is informal. The venue is not a formal lecture theatre, but a large room where some of the twenty or so students are sitting on cushions on the floor. I recognise some library staff members, and a few people from the maintenance staff. I take a deep breath, then talk for about twenty minutes. The address goes off well. Afterwards there are some questions – about diet, drug regimens – and then Dr Orr sums up and thanks me.

Afterwards, she mentions that she was particularly touched by my comment that I had always imagined myself having children and sitting at the head of a table for Sunday lunch, but now I would have to come to terms with the fact that this would not happen. She says the talk went well, and I feel relieved.

The group disperses. Some come up to thank me, telling me how inspiring they found the talk. Their words warm me. And then a young black woman in a denim jacket comes up to me with a beaming face. She mentions that she is a fourth-year law student, and the pang of fear in the pit of my stomach resurfaces. What if my students hear I have AIDS? Will they still register for the courses I teach? Will they want to be taught by someone who is possibly going to die soon? But I don my mask and smile, saying to her, 'Oh that's great. What subjects are you doing? Pop in sometime if you need help with your assignments – my office is downstairs.' Then I scuttle away.

And indeed the next day my phone rings. It is late afternoon.

'Good afternoon, Prof,' says the familiar voice. 'I was at your talk yesterday.' Then she continues, 'Can I come and see you? I am just upstairs.'

'Oh yes, do,' I respond, wondering which of her assignments she needs help with. There is a knock on my door almost immediately. I am at my cluttered desk, and she stands on the other side, dressed in the same blue jacket, gazing intently at me. She says, 'I am also HIV-positive.'

My office seems to rock like a plane, dipping up and down on its wingtips. I stumble up to her and give her an awkward hug, wanting to embrace her. But I hold back, having just seen a play about the ramifications of an academic getting involved with female students. Still, I feel very close to her. I wave to her to sit down, and take a big breath. A stream of facts comes pouring out across the desk at me. She was diagnosed earlier in the year, but she cannot tell her parents, who live in Soweto. They sent her to a Sandton clinic in the June–July vacation for treatment for her depression; she had been given electro-convulsive therapy. She has not told anybody about her status – not her parents, or her friends, or Dr Wendy Orr, or the therapist she is seeing. She has not obtained all her DPs (Duly Performed certificates) for her law assignments and does not qualify to write the final examinations. She is desperate and alone. She mirrors my own isolation.

I need to breathe and suggest going for a walk. We drive to nearby Kirstenbosch Gardens. It's late afternoon by now, and we head up the hill. Other walkers are coming down. In their averted glances I can see them asking what this middle-aged white guy is doing, walking up the mountain with a young black woman. Later, as I drop her at Liesbeeck Gardens, a converted block of flats that is now a student residence, I say to her, 'We're in the same boat. I'll keep in touch.' And I do.

A week or two later, on a Friday night, I come back home after being at a party. It's past midnight, and a light is blinking next to my bed. 'It's me, Prof,' says a raspy recorded voice. 'There's no point in living... I have taken some pills.' Uncharacteristically, I don't panic. Maybe it's the booze I had at the party. I picture the scene at Medical

Casualty at Groote Schuur, where I'd often been on a Friday night to get the nursing sister to put up my drip before we used concentrated factor VIII. There will be people milling in the corridor, harassed porters pushing trolleys, stab-wound victims groaning in the admission queue. I visualise the young woman lying on a bed, a screen around her, having her stomach pumped. I sit on my bed for a moment, then pull the covers down, and fall into a fitful sleep.

Next morning first thing, I phone Medical Casualty. Yes, they had had a Ms M there. She has been sent to Valkenberg Hospital for observation. I visit her that afternoon. She beams as she sees me. We have a short, awkward chat. She will be out soon. Her law exams are coming up. I promise to help her 'spot' the questions. 'You must give it your best shot,' I say. She promises to try. She is discharged a day or two later and does indeed seem to settle down to study. I am pleased.

About a month later, I attend the final Law Faculty board meeting of the year. Though tedious, it is a most important event, where twenty or thirty of us scrutinise each student's computer-generated mark and debate whether borderline students should be given a supplementary exam, readmitted, or even awarded a first. I check almost immediately how Ms M did – the Fs leap up at me. Fail, Pass, Fail, Fail, Pass read her five subjects. I listen to the drawn-out debates about whether certain students should qualify for a supplementary exam on compassionate grounds. One had a migraine on the day of the exam, another's granny died the day before. I wait anxiously for Ms M's entry to be reviewed. The chair eventually arrives, and tea and biscuits are served on a trolley.

In a flash, the young woman's fate is decided: 'Out: nowhere near a borderline case.'

But she is HIV-positive, I want to scream. With a sinking feeling in the pit of my stomach, I turn to the senior black lecturer next to me. 'Do you know this student?' I ask.

'Yes. She's a bit mad,' he says, then applies his mind to the next name on the computer-generated list.

A year or so later, I obtain her phone number through the faculty office and phone her. Her voice sounds sparky, she tells me she is on medication, she is fine, and is working in a supermarket in downtown Johannesburg. I am happy to hear the news.

CHAPTER 8

Entering Ukraine

IN OCTOBER 2004, armed with maps I had bought at Stanfords in London, which claims to be 'the world's biggest and best map shop', I flew to Warsaw. Here I had arranged to join my maternal cousin Paweł, his daughter Ewa, and her fiancé, Gabriel, on what was to be my first trip into Ukraine. I was excited to be setting off with them on the next day, first to explore my ancestral town of Lviv, and then to travel through the countryside to Chmielowa, site of my grandfather's manor house. At the back of my mind was the intention of returning sometime in the future to undertake an extensive search for the family silver, which my father had buried before fleeing Poland at the start of World War II.

I had always imagined that Chmielowa was the name of the estate that my father talked about – in the same way that Vygeboom was the name of the farm outside Durbanville. On the eve of our departure to Ukraine, I spread out the maps I had bought on the kitchen table, to discuss our route. After a minute or so, Paweł, who could read Cyrillic, exclaimed, 'Here is Chmielowa!' It suddenly dawned on me that Chmielowa was the name of the village, and that the name was used interchangeably by my father to refer to both the village and the family estate.

Although the Soviet government had collapsed more than a decade previously, Ukraine, as I correctly suspected, still had the lingering reek of communism about it. I first sensed this at the consulate in Pretoria, where I had to bypass stern-faced, armed guards to obtain a visa. (A few years later I was to obtain a Polish passport and so subsequently no longer needed to apply for visas.) In the austere waiting room, I signed a book of condolences for Ukrainian miners who had died in a recent accident that I had not even heard about. I then filled in a plethora of forms and eventually was granted a visa by a stony-faced official.

At last we are packing Gabriel's van outside the Dom Poselsky hotel, adjacent to the Polish parliament, our designated meeting point. It is an overcast but warm autumn morning. I have trouble containing my excitement. As we navigate through Warsaw's morning traffic, I calculate that, at an average speed of 100 kilometres per hour, we'll reach Lublin, halfway to the Ukrainian border, in time for morning tea. I tell this to my companions.

'No,' says Gabriel, the driver, 'we first have to stop at a scrapyard. The radiator developed a leak during my holiday in Italy.'

I suppress my frustration. We eventually find a car scrap centre on the outskirts of Warsaw and I surprise myself with my patient attitude. Perhaps that mindfulness meditation course I did a few months back in Cape Town was of some use after all.

We don't succeed in getting a replacement radiator but instead patch the existing one. We leave after two long hours and reach Lublin by lunchtime. Then on to the next large town, Zamość, where we walk around the beautiful old market square in the town centre. I take pictures of my cousins, and with Gabriel's smartphone we email them to my sister Wanda back in South Africa. I read in my *Lonely Planet* guidebook that this area teemed with Jewish people prior to World War II, and as we stroll around the central square, I can almost hear the merchants plying their trade.

We are on the road again, and I note with interest that the road signs indicating the distance to the town give the old Polish nomenclature,

Lwów, rather than the official Ukrainian Lviv. I wonder if still calling it Lwów is an indication of the Poles' persistent sentimental attachment to the town they'd lost after the war.

We are running much later than I expected. The prospect of leaving the European Union and entering a former communist country with a residual communist bureaucracy and heavy-handedness unnerves me. I'm not the only one. Tension mounts in the car when we get to the border. It's nearly nightfall. We get through the Polish side in about fifteen minutes. But then, for the next hour or so, we sit in a queue in the no-man's land between the Polish and Ukrainian sides.

Eventually our car pulls up alongside the Ukrainian customs control officials. The light in the kiosk casts an eerie silhouette on a sombre-uniformed woman as she saunters down to our car. I am reminded of war movies where tall blonde German women accost the hapless hero. She grabs the four passports from Gabriel's outstretched hand, three Polish and my South African one. She flips through the first three nonchalantly. But my passport seizes her intense gaze and clearly interests her. It is not often that a South African with a Polish surname crosses the border. She disappears back to the kiosk, passports in hand. The wait seems interminable, though she returns after twenty minutes.

'Pan Paweł,' she calls out briskly.

My cousin shouts: 'To ja!'

The official is satisfied that his face matches the passport photograph. The same procedure is repeated with Ewa and Gabriel. Then it is my turn.

'Pan Jan!'

'To ja,' I reply in the strongest voice I can muster.

'Where were you born?' she rasps in Polish, squinting at my passport in the fading light.

'In South Africa,' is my reply. I recollect uneasily that my father had unlawfully left this part of what was then Poland, with no papers.

'When were you born?' she rasps. I tell her 1953, even though it is all there in the visa attached to my passport, which she is holding with her thick fingers.

'Where are you going?'

'To Lwów,' I respond, thinking of all the road maps next to me where I have marked the route to Chmielowa, about 200 kilometres deeper into Ukraine.

'Why are you going there?'

'Tourista,' I respond, thinking of my grandfather's grave, which is hardly on the tourist map.

We are eventually waved through, though I am exasperated because Gabriel has to stop once again to purchase car insurance and check his leaking radiator.

But we are in Ukraine, and I am happy, although by now it is getting dark.

We reach Lwów after an hour or so. First impressions on the outskirts of the town are disappointing: rows of nondescript industrial buildings and plain houses. But as we reach the centre, the cityscape changes. There are wide cobbled streets, with trams rattling along in the middle. We must find Gabriel's friend's parents, and although he has been there before, he cannot remember the way. Their home is in Kotlarewśkoho Street.

A twofold problem arises. Firstly, the street names were changed when Lwów became Lviv after World War II, and so the street names to which my father referred in his instructions are no more. Secondly, the street signs are all in Cyrillic and I cannot decipher them. I abandon my usual inclination to navigate and leave it to Paweł, preferring simply to absorb the ambience of my father's and grandfather's home town. My cousins are not proficient in Russian, similar to Ukrainian, which they were reluctantly obliged to learn at school. I'm reminded of Soweto in 1976, when children rose up against an oppressive state because of a directive that they be taught in Afrikaans. Gabriel asks a pedestrian for directions and I gain some satisfaction from the fact that I can understand, more or less, his response. Ukrainian Polish sounds similar to the Polish I'm familiar with, though it is a lot more nasal.

After a frustrating hour, we reach Kotlarewśkoho Street and the home of the Tyssons, an elderly couple. Gabriel is a friend of their 28-year-old daughter, who'd studied in Poland with him. But she and her mother are not yet back from a week-long holiday in Crimea. We are greeted by the elderly and bedraggled Mr Tysson, who looks as if he's stepped out of a pre-war movie. He has lived in the house since well before the war, and it appears that nothing has changed. We admire a set of mahogany stairs leading to his lounge, where we are shown fold-out couches. We marvel at the ancient brass gas geyser in the bathroom, which had been heating their water since before World War II.

Over a cup of black tea I refer to my father's instructions and note, 'Once in Lwów you might be interested to see the house during my school days. Nabielaka No. 1...' I ask Mr Tysson if Nabielaka is nearby. This is the old Polish name for the street where my father lived as a boy. To my surprise Mr Tysson tells me that I am in Nabielaka. Its new name is Kotlarewśkoho. I am overwhelmed by the fact that I arrive in a city of three-quarters of a million people, and I find myself in the very street where my father had lived more than sixty years before. Maybe his spirit is guiding me. I go to bed tired but satisfied.

Next morning, I saunter up the cobbled street, watching out for the occasional rickety tram in the middle lane, and easily locate the paternal home. I am surprised at its size, a large double-storey with a spacious garden. A Cyrillic sign on the gate clearly indicates 'No Entry'. I nevertheless ring the bell hanging there, and a dishevelled, grumpy-looking man appears at the front door. I holler in Polish that my father lived here before the war, but he slams the door shut, probably suspecting that I have come to reclaim the house.

A second priority on arrival in Lwów was to locate my grandfather's grave. It was in Lwów that *Dziadzio* Adam spent the post-war years, after being banished from his Chmielowa estate by the Soviets. He lived in this impregnable town behind the Iron Curtain until he died in the early 1960s. The date of his death remains unclear. I recollect my father getting a letter informing him that his father had died, followed by another soon after, contradicting this.

Being unfamiliar with the town, we took a taxi instead of walking half an hour to the beautifully laid-out Łyczakowski Cemetery, a Unesco World Heritage Site. My French cousins had been there previously and had given me a rough idea of the grave's location in the vast cemetery. After twenty minutes I found the site and was pleasantly surprised to find fresh flowers there, four decades after his death. The date of *Dziadzio*'s death on the headstone was barely legible, but appeared to be 1960. I was further surprised to see that *Dziadzio* Adam was not alone in his grave. He was buried beside his own father, Ignacy, which is my second name, and two others, Leon and Leona Paszkowski. The latter names meant nothing to me, but on rereading my father's memoir, I learned that Leona was my father's aunt.

Although I can speak rudimentary Polish, I cannot write the language, and so, prompted by the fresh flowers, I left a note in English in a plastic wrapper, saying that I was Adam's grandson. I also left my address in Cape Town, but I never received a response. Years later my French cousin Adam, who insists that our grandfather died in 1962, commissioned the grave's restoration, and the headstone now states his date of death as 1962. My father's memoir gives 1960.

A further priority in Lviv was to discover the Armenian Cathedral with its murals by the Polish-born artist Jan Henryk de Rosen, which were completed in 1929. I'm not particularly knowledgeable about art, but my mission was to see my *Strij* Andrzej, whose image appears in these murals. During his late teens, he'd posed as a model for de Rosen. I was somewhat in awe viewing my uncle's image on the walls of a sacred place that dates back to the fourteenth century, itself modelled on the eleventh-century Armenian Cathedral in Ani, in today's Turkey.

Later I was to learn that de Rosen, being Jewish, was barred from painting in the Roman Catholic church in Lwów. Ironically, Pope Pius XI commissioned de Rosen to paint murals in his private chapel and summer residence at Castel Gandolfo, southeast of Rome. When Polish Pope John Paul II visited Ukraine in 2001, he insisted on having a ceremony at the Armenian Cathedral in Lviv. He also honoured the victims of the Holocaust as well as those who endured the Russian terror.

Lwów was always known as the third corner of the 'cultural capitals triangle', the other two being Vienna and Cracow. But it has also been a town of endless conflict and tumult, as evidenced by its various names. It was founded in the thirteenth century, and initially known as Leopolis (Leo's town) in honour of Lev, the king of Galicia, then situated on the border between today's Poland and Ukraine. During the time of the Austro-Hungarian Empire it became Lemberg; in the interwar period it was Lwów, in Poland; after World War II it became Lvov under the USSR; it remained Lvov when Russia re-emerged in the early 1990s. Today it is Lviv in Ukraine. It strikes me that my grandfather lived in a city that changed its name three times during his life.

But, to me, the town will always be Lwów, the name etched in my bones and embedded in my heart since childhood. I love Adam Zagajewski's poem 'Jechać do Lwowa' (Travel to Lwów), whose opening lines have been translated as follows:

> To go to Lwów. Which station
> for Lwów, if not in a dream, at dawn, when dew
> gleams on a suitcase, when express
> trains and bullet trains are being born.

To this day, the mention of faraway Lwów stirs up all kinds of feelings in me. It is the mysterious place where my forefathers came from; it is in my genes. The word 'solastalgia' comes to mind: though it has been defined in different ways, my favourite is 'the feeling of homesickness you have when you are still at home'.

*

Later I was to take a walk to the city's historic centre and was struck by the number of cathedrals and other places of worship that recall the city's diverse communities: Polish, Jewish, Ukrainian, Armenian and German. I marvelled at the majestic opera house in Svobody Avenue. I learned from my guidebook that it was built at the end of the eighteenth century and is an excellent example of Renaissance Revival architecture. I paused at the salmon-pink George Hotel in the centre of town, which my father had told us about over supper at Vygeboom. It seemed to me the local equivalent of Cape Town's stately Mount Nelson Hotel. It was no doubt at the George where *Dziadzio* and, later, my father would have met their friends and business associates for schnapps.

*

About a decade later I was to return to Lwów and learned more about the terrible atrocities committed by the Nazis during the Holocaust. A town with over thirty synagogues on the eve of World War II, it was left with only one in 1945. During the war, people were forced to shelter in the sewers. On my visit I went on one of the regular city bus tours. When we drove through the area that had once been the Jewish ghetto, all that the tour guide told us was that it was now the town's industrial area.

I was riveted by Philippe Sands's remarkable book *East West Street: On the Origins of Genocide and Crimes against Humanity*, published in 2016. It affected me profoundly. Apart from the fact that Lwów plays a central role in his story, the book focuses on two pre-eminent lawyers, Hersch Lauterpacht and Raphael Lemkin, both Lvóvians who had attended the city's Jan Kazimierz University (now Ivan Franko University) as students between the two world wars. This was shortly before Jews were excluded from that university. Lauterpacht played a central role in getting the notion of 'crimes against humanity' embedded in international law by introducing the concept at the Nuremberg trials, while Lemkin introduced the concept of genocide into the legal lexicon.

On this later trip to the town, I was privileged to accompany a group led by Sands to the village of Żółkiew where East West Street, after which Sands's book is named, is located. A busload of us, which included descendants and friends of Lauterpacht and Lemkin, headed from Lviv to the village from which their forebears had disappeared during the Holocaust. Here we visited Hersch Lauterpacht's birthplace.

We were also given permission to enter a perfectly ordinary suburban house in East West Street, which the occupants kindly made available for our visit. We were led to the main bedroom, where the carpet next to the bed had been pushed aside and a few floorboards lifted, revealing rickety wooden steps leading to the dim underfloor area. This was where eighteen people had hidden in a bunker dug out of the basement. An SS officer who was billeted in the house realised that some Jews were hiding there but turned a blind eye. Clara Kramer kept a diary during the twenty terrifying months she spent in hiding with the others. She survived, and subsequently wrote a book, *Clara's War*, about the trauma of her experience.

We stared into the cramped space below. Some climbed down. It all felt quite surreal.

We then proceeded by bus to a nearby field, surrounded by young forest growth, where some 3 500 Jews were executed. We spent a sombre time there, silently contemplating the scene. Afterwards we sat down together, discussing the alleged collaboration by local Ukrainians with the Nazis, noting that in some villages the collaborators could well have been Poles.

Top: Kids from the Polish community with whom I grew up (me with shoes in the middle).

Bottom: My widowed father with four children married Kathleen Edwards, a widow with eight children, in January 1962. Here are the twelve of us with the priest who married them. I am seated second from right.

Right: Andrzej and Adela, Layla's mother, the two children of the new marriage, circa 1968.

Right: My father and stepmother were happy to see me graduate in 1976 (with a BCom LLB).

Right: My 40th birthday party with my sisters, Krysia, Marysia (Mish) and Wanda.

Top: Grandfather's pre-war townhouse in Lviv. It is still there today.

Bottom: The barn on Chmielowa marked on my father's map, still standing after 80 years.

Top left: Chmielowa 2019. The 94-year-old *Pani* Paulina, who knew my *Dziadzio*.

Top right: Chmielowa 2019. A woman in her vegetable garden with sugar beets.

Bottom: Chmielowa 2019. Taras with the 'radar' detector.

The silver buried in 1939, found in 2019.

Top left: First glint of silver.

Top right: A jewelry box, probably packed hurriedly by my mother in 1939.

Bottom left: Some of the hoard.

Bottom right: Layla with a candelabra.

Left: The christening spoon with my father's name engraved on it.

Right: Me at the excavation happy to have found the silver.

Right: Departing Chmielowa with the forest in the background.

Top: 'Farming' in McGregor. Among other things I grow artichokes in my vegetable patch.

Left: My wife, Louise, with one of our four chickens that produces four eggs daily.

Top: A trip to Antarctica in 2008 with my haematologist, Dr Mike du Toit.

Bottom: With my 12-year-old grand-nephew John, also a haemophiliac, and his older brother, Danny, visiting Robben Island in 2022. Improved treatment methods will mean he will not have all the joint problems that I have experienced.

Entering Ukraine

Our guide in Żółkiew was an intrepid local woman named Ludmilla, who worked in the village heritage office. She had done much to unearth the ugly history of the village, and was not popular with the locals for doing so.

Philippe Sands has poignantly observed that many people come to Lviv to regain their identity. His remark has stayed with me.

*

But let us go back to my first trip to Ukraine in 2004. After a day or two we leave Lviv, struggling to find the exit route leading to Chmielowa. Although I have my father's much-fingered instructions in my hand, I abandon any attempt at navigating (this was before the era of Google Maps), even though I am in the passenger's seat: the street signs – where they exist – are in Cyrillic. In any event my father anticipated that I would going by train, not by road. The way out of the city seems remarkably unclear. I'm astonished by the fact that the main route out of such a big city is a very narrow cobbled road. It winds through industrial sites and grubby apartment blocks, where children play in the road – clearly the poorer side of town.

Suddenly we are out of Lwów and the landscape changes dramatically. We drive through green, hilly country, with a gorge on the right where we stop for a short leg-stretch. My trip to Chmielowa is now real. I remember my father's instruction to 'change the train in Stanisławow' – now renamed Ivano-Frankivsk. I clutch my two road maps and follow the route quite easily; I have no trouble deciphering the Cyrillic sign showing Stanisławow, aided by the fact that the map is bilingual. We bypass the town. I remember my father saying that the route then goes through the villages of Brzezany, Podhajce and Monasterzyska, names that I can decipher with Ewa's help.

The big skies, the black earth, the geese scattering as we drive through muddy villages, a peasant woman standing staring alongside a tethered cow – all this reminds me of rural Africa. And yet I am in western Ukraine. The landscape captivates me: flat, with big blue skies and huge white rolling clouds. It has rained heavily, just an hour or two ago, and I can smell the fetid earth. This was, at least until the Russian invasion in 2022, the 'bread basket of Europe'. I think of my father's note, 'Approach to Farming', which I found among his papers in the concertina file I inherited from him. In it, he emphasised that caring for the land is an intergenerational activity, that the family plays a major role in determining agricultural productivity.

I take in the landscape of flat fields and rolling hills, dotted with people involved in the seasonal activity of growing hay. The tarred road is in good condition yet relatively quiet. We come to an intersection where we slow down to check our directions. A horse-drawn cart clops by; seated in it are a craggy-faced, dark-skinned couple. I pick up my newly acquired digital camera to take a picture with some hesitation, remembering how annoyed some rural Africans become when I want to photograph them. This couple, however, seem amused that someone wants to photograph them, and they break into peals of laughter. As they pass by, I see the husband giving the wife an affectionate hug.

We drive through villages where people walk in the street with goats and cows. We are careful to avoid the geese, which are gathered in flocks. Cousin Paweł informs me that each flock of geese returns in the evening to their rightful owner, much like homing pigeons. My father's instructions were to 'take the train to Buczacz', which we reach by road in the late afternoon. It is dominated by the pre-war town hall towering over the central square. This is the town where my father said I should disembark. I wonder how he thought I was going to travel the remaining thirty or forty kilometres to Chmielowa. By now we are hungry, and we stroll around the striking town, where we buy sausages and bread rolls.

From Buczacz, the instructions are: 'take the road towards Jazłowiec... situated deep in a valey (*sic*) you climb the main road, pass on your right the convent of the sisters of immaculate conception with a sharp bend to the left.' My father went on to note that Jazłowiec was some fifteen kilometres beyond Buczacz.

Some years before, in London, when I described this route to *Ciocia* Ala, who was then in her late eighties, she exclaimed, 'No, not fifteen, it was eighteen kilometres further on.' She went on to recount how, some sixty years before, she used a horse and carriage to travel from Buczacz station to Jazłowiec. This was the village where she attended school, the convent of the Siostry Niepokalanego (Sisters of the Immaculate Conception), which she clearly loved as much as any young person could love a boarding school. Before we'd left Lwów, cousin Ewa phoned the convent to book an overnight stay, as there are no regular places of accommodation or shops in Jazłowiec or Chmielowa. During the communist era all the Catholic churches and convents had been suppressed, some being converted to health spas, but by now many had revived.

It is nearly nightfall, and we explore a crumbling cathedral before moving on to the convent. Transformed into a spa by the previous communist rulers, it has now been restored to its former simple beauty. The quietly spoken nun in her grey-and-white habit serenely shows us to our rooms and politely invites us to a communal supper in the dining room. As I leave my suitcase on my narrow bed, I wonder whether this may have been *Ciocia* Ala's room decades before. The convent grounds are beautifully restored after years of neglect. We take a pre-supper walk along a wooded road to the nuns' burial ground, where each grave has its own stone and plaque.

Next day, after a light breakfast, we give the nuns an offering in lieu of a formal payment and set off for Chmielowa, a mere ten kilometres away.

'Follow the main road and turn off to the right about 2–3 kilometres from the convent towards Beremiany [Brezeżany] but instead turning to the right towards that village you carry on straight another couple of kilometres.'

We are not sure that we are on the right road, but we forge ahead. I marvel once again at how flat and black the earth is, set against the blue sky. In the distance I see a dip and surmise that this must be the Dniester River, which flows into the Black Sea and on whose banks Chmielowa is situated. Again, I recollect *Ciocia* Ala's nostalgia as she recounted how, during their youth, she and her siblings would canoe on the water, often stopping to enjoy refreshments in Chmielowa.

'Go through a small valey [*sic*] and then turn to the right towards Chmielowa. Just before you reach the village you pass the village cemetery on the right. Carrying on straight Cerkiew (Greko Catholic Church).' We are at last nearing our destination. The Greek Orthodox Church with its adjacent cemetery provides a reliable landmark – we seem to be on the right track. My heart is beating faster, although I feign nonchalance. 'And you still carry on strait [*sic*] few hundred metres after passing the cerkiew, you enter the gate of the folwark (farm buildings) Chmielowa (see pencil drawn map).'

We have arrived! I'm at the precise spot where my father and my pregnant mother left in a hurry some sixty years previously, their lives in upheaval. I recognise a farm building from family photographs. We get out of the car and wander around. My first impression is that I am stepping on flat green clover, with the Dniester River drifting leisurely by in the valley below, and the village of Chmielowa now behind us. Remarkably, the land is not cultivated. A lone cow munches clover where my father may have grown his Brussels sprouts before the war. The manor house is no longer there. I try to work out where the house may have been, and eventually Paweł discovers the foundations as well as the cellar, which is still largely intact. My father had spoken about the cellar, where he stored his vegetables before taking them to the weekly market at Zaleszczyki.

I marvel at the view from what would have been the home's terrace, which is clearly indicated on my father's map. I take a few pictures and note that this particular view is exactly the same as the one in the photograph that had hung in our lounge ever since my childhood. We amble across to the edge of the farm. On the left, the forested land slopes down to the river, with red, gold and russet trees basking in the autumn sunshine, while on the right the land is flat and a cow stands unperturbed by our presence. I gasp, astounded at the beauty of the terrain. I capture the scene on my cell phone while Gabriel also takes pictures of me on 'my land'.

An old woman on the village side of the farm wanders across to us. My cousin is immediately nervous. 'Are you a Glazewski?' she asks.

'Yes,' I reply, taken aback. Then I ask, 'Did you know my father?'

'No, I was moved here after the war,' she answers in a mix of Polish and Ukrainian. She tells me she has heard about me from my late father's coachman, who died a few years before. I feel regret that I did not meet this man.

We speculate where the treasure might be: 'on the left side of the pencil drawn map you will see the broken line going from the stone wall towards the forest (oaks)'. I gaze at the distant forest, which gently slopes towards a tributary of the Dniester that is some 200 metres wide. But I have difficulty in correlating the crudely drawn map with what I see before me all these years after my father was there, and so I suggest returning next year. My thinking is that we could scan the ground with a metal detector, unseen by inquisitive villagers. I gather a few stones and put them in my pocket to take back to South Africa as a memento.

A few weeks later I'm back in reality, in Cape Town, in the Law Faculty tea room, where I recount the story to Halton Cheadle, a leading human rights lawyer. He tells me about a recent European law case concerning a group of Polish people reclaiming land in former Poland and promises to get me a copy of the law report. It is now in my possession.

*

The following year, 2005, I am back in Chmielowa, this time with two of my older sisters, Wanda and Marysia, and their husbands. We've been exploring the farm for about an hour now and have spread out a bit. The muddy, brown Dniester wends its way languidly below us, hardly seeming to move as it makes its way to the Black Sea. Gabriel is busily trying to rid his Kombi of a swarm of midges that welcomed us with noisy buzzing as the vehicle bumped to a halt on the farm. I feel the sun on my back and notice a stooped old man and his dog crossing the farm some distance away. He sees me ambling over, changes direction, and comes my way.

'Dzien dobry,' I say, wishing him a good day. I notice his piercing blue eyes, gold-capped front tooth, and his working boots. He responds warmly and asks about my presence here. 'My name is Glazewski, my family lived here many years ago, before the war...' I begin in Polish.

'Ah, Glazewski...' His eyes light up. 'How wonderful...I remember your father...'

'No, grandfather,' I say, although it could well have been my father, who had by then taken over and begun farming the land. 'My parents worked for him,' he continues, animated. 'They paid them two złoty a day and me one złoty as I was only twelve years old.'

I beckon to my sisters, who are gathering some flowers that have popped out of the field here and there. He immediately takes a shine to Marysia, telling her how beautiful she is. They chat away about what was where on the farm, and about our father and our grandfather.

'Yes,' he says, 'when the Russians came they wanted to kill your grandfather. But my parents and the other workers said, "No, let him be. He is a good man." They flattened the house, saying it was a symbol of capitalism.' This was done to all the *mająteks* (manor houses) in the district. It is not unlike what is happening in Zimbabwe, where the houses of white farmers are being razed to the ground or occupied by locals – such is the thought that comes to my mind.

'Why don't you come back?' His eyes glint mischievously. 'Come and farm, though it was much better in those days.'

I imagine rebuilding the house, sitting on the veranda after a long day in the fields, sipping steaming hot broth while watching the waters of the Dniester glide slowly by, and listening to the workers chattering in the sunset on their way home.

I come back from my reverie, and his voice drifts over to me.

'Yes, my son is now in Kyiv,' he is saying to my sister Wanda. 'Life is difficult there, though not as hard as here. He can find some jobs.' But I sense he has lost touch with his son, who has disappeared into the industrial heartland. I also sense a longing in him as he sets off down the hill, stick in hand, idly swishing at the ankle-high grass. Or is it my longing? His scrawny brown dog bounds along beside him.

*

Some of the old people in the village remembered my father and grandfather, whom they referred to as the 'landlord on the hill'. Some would have traipsed up the small incline to work on the estate. *Dziadzio*, who worked in Lwów, retired early in the 1930s and went to live on the Chmielowa estate, which he had inherited. My father started farming here a few years before the war broke out. He grew vines and bottled his own wine. To this day, the framed wine labels hang proudly on my study wall. But then came the war...

Dziadzio refused to leave his estate, despite protestations from his four sons, who encouraged him to head for Cracow. This was his place, and he had survived World War I, so why leave? He'd rather face head-on whatever was coming. My father's mini-memoir recounts: 'He was immediately arrested and led by a Russian patrol to a nearby forest, which was planted by him some thirty years earlier, to be shot as the landowner and enemy of the people. Many peasants, who quickly learned of the arrest, were following the Russian patrol, and after some discussions persuaded them to let my father free.'

This account was verified on a subsequent visit by *Pani* Paulina, a very old lady who lived in the village. She told us that, shortly before the Russian army arrived, they had tried to hide *Dziadzio* from the Russian soldiers. However, he was found, and was about to be executed along with other Polish landowners in the area. But the peasants persuaded the would-be executioners that he was a good man and that he should not be shot. They agreed, provided that he did not go back to the manor house, which was destroyed soon afterwards by the Russian army.

Dziadzio then made his way back to Lwów, probably by horse and cart. My father's memoir continues: 'In Lwow for his first meal he had to sell the gold cuff-links from his shirt.' Although he was to live another twenty years or more, neither my father nor his three brothers were ever to see my grandfather again. Again, my father recounts how after the war they had to correspond through an intermediary: 'I was sending my letters to an address in Istanbul where it was put into another enveloppe [*sic*] and posted to Lwow under German or Russian occupation.'

In Lwów my grandfather continued his pre-war association with the Catholic church of St Mary Magdalene. Using his legal training, he negotiated with the communists and managed to survive the oppressive Stalin years. When, during my student days in London, I visited *Ciocia* Tychna, who by that time had left South Africa, she recounted that, on *Dziadzio*'s death, the church wanted to erect a monument in his memory to acknowledge the efforts he put into maintaining the building and acting as a go-between for the congregation and the new communist rulers. On one of my later trips to Lwów, with the help of a local guide, I located an elderly church official who remembered *Dziadzio*, and in the archives I found church committee documents containing his name.

After the war, the Chmielowa estate was converted into a collective farm by the Soviets. It was probably run by the same villagers who had worked for *Dziadzio*.

CHAPTER 9

Finding Louise

I WOKE up completely despondent and low-spirited, and struggled to get out of bed to start my working day. The feeling had been there for over a week. As I sat on the edge of my bed contemplating the emptiness of my life, I reached for my bedside phone and rang an old friend I'd met in my Johannesburg days.

'Trish, I can't go on,' I burst out as she picked up the phone.

She was aware of my situation, but said, 'Jan, I cannot do anything for you…'

But, unbeknown to me, she *did* do something. A few days later I received a call from my niece Michaela, who suggested a walk in Newlands Forest at five on Thursday afternoon. I readily joined her and learned that she regularly walked with her dogs, and her daughter in a pram, while her son was at swimming lessons with his dad. From then on, I routinely accompanied Michaela every Thursday. We chatted while she pushed her child, following a regular circuit.

Once, she tentatively asked me, 'What would you like, Jan, a friend, a lover – or what?' The question took me aback. Avoiding a direct answer, I mumbled something like 'a good friend, perhaps'.

I enjoyed our Thursday walks. We'd sometimes bump into her running mate, Louise, coming in the opposite direction, walking her two dogs. I would stand idly by, admiring her friend's short silver-grey hair, clear features and lithe figure, as the two women laughed and talked, usually about their training for their big challenge, the Two Oceans Ultra Marathon, which they planned to run the following year.

For some inexplicable reason this 'chance' meeting happened every Thursday. One of Louise's dogs, Suzie, was always straining at her leash, while the other, Rolo, was free to sniff around the forest. Eventually I could not contain myself any longer. The very first words I said to Louise were: 'Do you have to keep that dog on such a tight leash?' The words proved prophetic!

The next time we met on our regular walks, it was late afternoon and I engineered an invitation for soup at her house down the road from Newlands Forest. Rolo, a rather stocky cross between a corgi and a mysterious other, insisted on manoeuvring himself onto my lap as I was sitting on an easy chair in the kitchen while Louise examined soup recipe books. The stage was set.

A few weeks later, while Michaela and I were walking along the Newlands Forest route, who should come in the opposite direction but Louise with Suzie and her beloved Rolo. After a brief exchange of pleasantries, I continued down the hill. But this time, much to Louise's chagrin, Rolo followed me. It was then that she realised Rolo needed a 'father' – and her sights were set on me. Soon thereafter, Michaela invited us both to a cricket test match at Newlands. It was a normal working day and the weather was not great. I nearly bailed out but I am glad I didn't.

That was autumn 2011. I was 58 at the time, eight years older than Louise, and I had found an answer to Michaela's question. Although we'd both had previous relationships, neither of us had been married, nor did we have any children. Perhaps this is why we have a common love for dogs, which are now our constant companions.

*

Around that time, a law colleague who'd specialised in energy law invited me to attend a public meeting on hydraulic fracturing, or 'fracking'. Although I did not really know what fracking was, I vaguely recollected a climate conference in Poland where two highly excitable Poles accosted me in a corridor and explained how harmful some proposed gas extraction activity was to the environment. The public meeting was to be held at Kelvin Grove, an elite Cape Town club, which suggested that a large segment of the Cape Town community, including people from the surrounding townships, would not be able to attend.

I entered a hall abuzz with excitement and listened to two besuited gentlemen from Shell South Africa trying to explain their proposal to undertake hydraulic fracturing in the Karoo. I learned this would entail injecting millions of litres of water mixed with fracking fluids deep underground, with the resultant pressure splitting the rocks so as to release the gas. The attendees were not impressed, and the presenters were barracked by the boisterous audience. There was also an impassioned anti-fracking talk from the renowned environmental activist Lewis Pugh – the 'Human Polar Bear' – who vowed in Churchillian tones, 'We will fight them all the way to the Constitutional Court.' At question time, the presenters were pressed to disclose what chemicals they would use in the process. They refused to name them on business grounds, and evaded questions about the key issue of water supply, going so far as to suggest a fluid that might be a substitute for fresh water, or pumping seawater or grey water from the Vaal sludge dams.

By the end of the meeting I was convinced that fracking in the Karoo should not take place. I put my head together with my law colleague as well as Susie Brownlie, a leading environmental sciencist and friend, and we cobbled together a twenty-page memorandum. I managed to get the report to Cabinet through a colleague on the National Planning Commission. Shortly thereafter the minister of mines, Susan Shabangu, announced a three-month moratorium on fracking so as 'to investigate the matter further'. The three months became three years, as a number of other parties investigated the issue, including the prestigious Academy of Science of South Africa (ASSAf). Eventually, after a thorough study by the Council for Scientific and Industrial Research (CSIR), the plan for fracking in the Karoo was shelved.

*

Soon after my introduction to the fracking issue at Kelvin Grove, I was chatting to a friend after the regular Sunday morning meditation session at the Temenos retreat centre in McGregor. She mentioned that she was about to set off to the region of Sikkim in India for a retreat, together with a group of local Buddhists. I had never heard of Sikkim but made a spontaneous decision to join the group at their ashram in the foothills of the Himalayas. First stop was Delhi, where we were fortunate to have an audience with His Holiness the Karmapa, who headed the Karma Kagyu, a school of Tibetan Buddhism that fell under the Dalai Lama, the highest spiritual leader of Tibet. This seemed all rather foreign, but the sentiments resonated with me. My main recollection of the few days we spent in Delhi in transit to Sikkim was the variety of pungent smells and the numerous homeless dogs roaming the streets.

I felt a little out of place in the presence of the holy people we met, but what I especially enjoyed was practising qigong in the early morning and playing cricket with young trainee monks on one of our off days. I was somewhat distracted during the more serious meditation and chanting sessions, and would send WhatsApp messages to Louise when we were in our rooms supposedly for individual meditation.

While there I made two important personal resolutions: the first was to marry Louise, and the second was to do my utmost to prevent fracking in the Karoo – both of which came to fruition. As I have mentioned already, the fracking project was shelved a few years later, and less than a year after meeting Louise, I asked her to marry me.

In October 2012, we had a memorable marriage ceremony in the Temenos garden, which was to become a very special place for me when we eventually retired to McGregor.

PART 3

Finding Silver... and Gold

CHAPTER 10

The Silver Beckons

IT IS Christmas Day immediately preceding my last year of work at the University of Cape Town. The university has been a ship carrying numerous passengers, including me, a colleague quipped, but I am relieved to be retiring soon as the last few years had become unpleasant, even toxic, after the Fees Must Fall events of 2015–2016. Louise and I are at her mother's house in Pinelands, a suburb of Cape Town, sharing in the family's traditional Christmas fare of pork belly, potatoes and vegetables with her brother and his two adult daughters.

I am given a novel by Louise's niece who works at the Book Lounge in the city. The book intrigues me. Its back cover tells me that it is set in Lviv. On the inside flap is a photograph of the author, Alina Jabłońska. I am struck by her mass of thick, tousled hair. The accompanying note states that she grew up in Lviv but now lives in Cracow, Poland, and that her debut novel has won an award.

I devour the novel. Among other things, I am taken by the names and descriptions of the streets and buildings, many of which my father had mentioned. It so happens that I am on sabbatical leave for the first half of my final year, and I plan to spend some of this time in the flat I now own in Cracow.

I google Alina Jabłońska but cannot find any contact details. So I contact my old friend Therese, who now lives in a village in France. Not only would she enjoy the book, as her father had a similar history to mine, but I also hope that she still has connections in Cracow, where she studied fine arts, who might know the author. A month or two later, I receive a WhatsApp message from Therese, who is visiting Paris: 'Well dear Janek!!!! Please sit down! I was 3/4 hrs. early, went to the Ksiegarnia Polska [Polish bookshop] Bld St. Germain and...the only person there was...Alina Jabłońska...She's expecting you to write to her so as to fix up a rendezvous with you, when you'll next be in Cracow...Your name is JANEK!!!'

It turns out that Alina was in France to participate in a book festival in Lyons. Passing through Paris, she was having coffee with her publisher and was persuaded rather reluctantly to pop in at the Polish bookshop. Therese was paying for her copy of Alina's new book when the cashier asked if she would like to meet the author, who had just walked in. Therese rushed to the stairs, and gasped, 'Are you Alina? There is a man from South Africa who wants to meet you!' Alina was intrigued that somebody 'from Africa' was interested in her book. She and Therese immediately formed a bond, and Alina ended up staying with her during the Lyons book festival, as Therese's home is in a village nearby.

On arrival in Cracow a few months later, I immediately set up a meeting with Alina. Declining my offer of tea and biscuits, she opted for coffee. 'Black,' she insisted.

'What a coincidence that you and Therese were in the Polish bookshop in Paris at the same time,' I said.

'There is no such thing as a coincidence,' she replied laconically in her Polish-Ukrainian accent.

I told her of my father's link to Lwów, hesitant as to whether it was politically correct still to be using the old Polish name for Lviv. I mentioned the name of the street where my father grew up, and to which he'd referred in his instructions. Not only did she recognise it immediately, but she also sent me a link to a site indicating all the old Polish street names and their current Ukrainian versions.

I contained my excitement when Alina mentioned she had a flat in Lviv that her friends used from time to time. I realised that I had established not only a wonderful Ukrainian-Polish connection, but also a possible base in Lwów to embark on my expedition to the rural hinterland. At one of our subsequent meetings in a coffee shop in Cracow's majestic Rynek (Central Square), I casually told her the story of the buried treasure, but she seemed only partly interested. Nevertheless, we'd formed a solid connection.

It was at one of our meetings that I suggested she attend the Franschhoek Literary Festival in the Cape. Since she was especially keen to see 'Africa', I duly contacted the festival organisers. I also arranged to have her book reviewed in the *Cape Times*. By good fortune, Therese decided to visit her childhood haunts during the same period.

Naturally, Alina would not travel all the way from Poland simply for the festival weekend, so I arranged a road trip for her after the event, together with Therese. After visiting a private game reserve on the edge of the Karoo which boasted 'the Big Five', and my home village of McGregor, we travelled to Rheenendal near Knysna where my youngest half-sister, Adela, and her daughter Layla live. Layla has a literary bent, and we had a spontaneous poetry evening, ending up singing Polish songs, although my recall became increasingly vague as the evening wore on. The next day we showed Alina the natural beauty of the Knysna area. The highlight, at least for me, was a visit to the Rastafarian community in Judah Square in the middle of the neighbouring township, the largest such community in the country. We were warmly received, as Layla's father had built a community hall there.

So taken was Alina with Layla and the Knysna experience that she reciprocated by inviting Layla and me on a road trip to Ukraine that would include the Carpathians. I happily accepted, and suggested that we include a search for my family's buried silver at Chmielowa.

The stage was set for me to fulfil a lifelong ambition.

*

The year 2019 was the first year of my retirement. I opted to start this new and potentially challenging stage of my life by having my right ankle replaced. That joint, like my elbow, my knee joints and my left ankle, had been severely damaged after years of recurrent internal bleeding. A new ankle would at least enable me to walk without pain. While I'd had the more conservative fusion procedure on my left ankle some twenty years previously, I now decided to have ankle replacement surgery. Though it was a largely untested procedure on haemophiliacs, I decided to give it a shot as it would provide me with more mobility than a fusion would. I was hoping to do more walking and hiking during my retirement years. The surgery itself was a success but, while recovering at a post-operative care facility, disaster struck.

It was a hot summer day, and the air-conditioner was turned on in my stuffy step-down facility ward. At around six that evening, I had just had one of my regular factor VIII transfusions, and suddenly I felt horribly cold. My teeth were chattering. I summoned the nurse aide to turn off the air-conditioner and called for blankets and a duvet, even though the heat of the day had not dissipated. She called the sister, who announced that my blood pressure was dangerously high – 200/150 – and my pulse was racing. I demanded that they call the doctor on duty, but he had already gone home. He eventually arrived after what felt like hours and, surmising that I'd had an allergic reaction to my infusion, he injected me with an antihistamine. This put me straight to sleep. I had a terrible nightmare that I was being held captive in my own house in McGregor while Louise was away on an excursion. I woke up a few hours later, completely disoriented, not knowing where I was or why I was in hospital.

The next day, I had my scheduled follow-up appointment with the surgeon. Louise collected me and we arrived early at the surgery. As I sat in a wheelchair in the waiting area with a few other patients, the surgeon walked through from his office to his procedure room. As he passed by and greeted me, he felt my clammy brow, took my pulse and instantly announced, 'Infection!' 'Limb-threatening,' were his chilling words. 'He must get to the hospital immediately.'

Louise drove me straight back to the UCT public-private hospital, where I was immediately put on intravenous antibiotics. I spent a miserable, solitary ten days in a viewless hospital ward with a seemingly endless procession of concerned doctors checking on my welfare. Eventually I was diagnosed with a bladder infection – in all probability, the result of a super-bug in the care facility.

I recovered after a few weeks and happily returned to McGregor, where, after a month or two, I was able to walk comfortably in the hills with our dogs, Rolo and Smartie.

During my recovery period, Louise made arrangements for us to join a guided architectural heritage trip to Rome organised by her mentor and colleague, as well as his wife. We would be accompanied by one of Louise's former heritage management master's classmates and her husband, making three couples in all. I was not keen, as my head was focused on my pending road trip to Ukraine with Alina and Layla.

Ultimately, I was a reluctant passenger to Rome, though I did enjoy our first days, becoming acquainted with such architectural gems as Bramante's Chiostro and with Caravaggio's paintings. After a few days, I abandoned the heritage aficionados, and went off on my own, crossing the Tiber and visiting the Botanical Gardens. On one of these wanderings I was delighted to discover South African artist William Kentridge's extensive, though fading, murals on the concrete embankment along the Tiber.

Louise and I returned to Cracow, where she was scheduled to board a return flight to Cape Town a few days later. She would not be joining me on my search, for this was my personal quest and I wanted to do it without her help. Besides, having *two* strong-willed women – Louise and Alina – as companions was more than I could cope with!

I was happy that Layla had arrived from Cape Town in an excited state and was overnighting with Alina and her family. This was her first trip to Poland, the land of her maternal ancestors.

In the days and weeks preceding my departure, doubts about the wisdom of the expedition increased, especially as the scheduled date of leaving grew closer. I felt that the likelihood of finding anything was minimal. In the first instance, I had never troubled to find out what the 'family silver' entailed; for all I knew, it could be a few spoons and teacups. Also, at the time it was secreted, the local farm workers would, in all probability, have noticed that items had been removed from the manor house and could, with the smallest of effort, have located the spot in the forest where the cache was buried, and dug it up themselves. The map itself was hardly a model of precision either. All in all, was there really any point? One positive aspect of the journey was that I would see a bit of Ukraine in the company of Layla. She had recently returned from her five years of travelling abroad after completing school, and I looked forward to getting to know her better and hearing about her adventures first-hand.

I had envisaged planning my final attempt to find the treasure with military precision. But the Rome trip had distracted me from my mission, and I had failed to plan at all. I was anxious and concerned that I had not made any firm arrangements or done any thorough research. I had left things largely to chance.

A further question that niggled me was, in the unlikely event that I did find something there, how would I transport it and where would I take it to? I doubted whether I could carry it across the border. Should I donate it to a museum; and was there a museum in Ukraine devoted to pre-World War II Polish artefacts? Again I had my doubts. I wondered if I could impose upon the Sisters of the Immaculate Conception in the nearby village of Jazłowiec, to whom my father had referred in his instructions. I had spent a night at the convent on my first trip to Chmielowa in 2004. The nuns could possibly safeguard any items until a plan was made. In short, I had no ready contacts in Ukraine with whom I could leave anything that I might find.

Of further concern was the question: what if I had an accident in Ukraine and needed extra life-saving blood-clotting factor? Because of its bulk, I normally carry only a limited supply. Would the Ukrainian hospitals be able to provide the blood product and treat me? Would they recognise my medical insurance?

The questions continued to pile up. What if the border authorities found a metal detector in my vehicle at the Polish–Ukrainian border crossing? Would that not raise some tricky questions? Though I considered whether to contact the Ukrainian authorities before embarking on the expedition, I had not done so as I wanted to avoid all bureaucratic hiccups. The stony-faced officials at Pretoria's Ukrainian consulate were bad enough, and I balked at trying to do this officially, navigating my way through Ukraine's impenetrable government departments. On top of that, there was the language problem: while ordinary Ukrainians seemed to understand my rudimentary Polish, trying to communicate and negotiate in Ukrainian would be an insurmountable barrier. In addition, the absurd notion occurred to me that if I approached the Ukrainian authorities, they themselves might try to find the buried silver. In any event, I reasoned that the treasure would simply be my parents' silverware, candlesticks, cutlery, teapots, and so on, of no great interest to anybody except perhaps an antique dealer. I was doing this purely for sentimental reasons and I told myself I would be happy to just find a silver teaspoon.

Yet despite all my doubts, I continued to fantasise about finding the treasure. I realised, however, that without a metal detector there was no chance of locating it. I thought of trying to obtain one in Poland – but how would I go about this? I had no connections in the geological world and no technical knowledge of metal detectors, or even of the type one needs to locate something buried a metre or so below the ground. I thought of contacting Clinton, my geologist friend from university residence days. He now lived in faraway Vancouver and was at that time away exploring in some remote part of northern Canada.

A week before our departure from South Africa, I had fired off an email to Alina, on the off-chance that she could source a metal detector. It seemed a remote possibility, as she mixes with people whose concerns are literature and poetry – I should instead be talking to geologists or engineers. But, lo and behold, she responded a few days later. Not only had she sourced a metal detector, but it belonged to a Ukrainian archaeologist named Taras. This gave me further comfort: I assumed that an archaeologist would have whatever permit was needed to explore and dig. The fact that he offered to accompany us to Chmielowa and provide us with his expertise was an added bonus. So, in one fell swoop several obstacles had been overcome, thanks to Alina. Not only had I found a qualified archaeologist with a metal detector, but also an expert with local knowledge and familiar with local conditions.

After Rome, I met Alina in Cracow to discuss logistics. I was disappointed to hear that she had only a week to spare for the road trip and had prepared an itinerary that focused on getting to the Carpathians, where she had booked a chalet for our group. She had also allocated only one day for a visit to the family estate. A lifelong dream to be carried out in one day! I persuaded her to increase it to at least two days.

The night before Alina was to collect Layla and me, I realised that I had left my father's map in Cape Town. Luckily, I had a copy of it on my computer. The next morning, before our departure, I hurried downstairs to have it printed at the copy shop below the flat. I realised that I had been focusing on the wrong things – for example, whether there would be enough provisions en route, as I become light-headed if I don't have a snack every few hours. Louise, who had not yet left for Cape Town, helped me pack and ensured that I did not leave anything behind this time.

At last we were ready to go. I was excited but apprehensive. The four of us – Alina, her sixteen-year-old son Marek, who had dyed his hair green, my niece Layla and I – set off in Alina's imposing-looking black Toyota Land Cruiser. Our first stop was a roadside petrol station and shop, and there I filled the brand-new flask bought by Louise with hot water to make tea. After setting off again, I noticed that the flask was leaking. In my anxious state, I had left the inner cap on the shop counter. I thought of asking Alina to turn back to retrieve it, but there were more important things ahead.

It is October 2019, and as we head east on the two-lane highway to the border, I muse about the fact that here I am, once again, on my way to my grandfather's estate. But this time I am with Layla. That's special for me. Our destination is Chmielowa, and this time I am not here for just a look-see but am excited to be making my first real attempt to find the silver buried by my father eighty years ago. After the border crossing, our first stop is Lwów, where we overnight in Alina's flat before continuing on to Chmielowa the next day. From there, it is about five hours to the former family estate.

En route, I consult my father's map and instructions and read for the hundredth time: 'You will find two Chmielowas, don't confuse our Chmielowa with the one on the other side of the river Dniester which has nothing to do with us.' In the meantime, Taras, our archaeologist with the metal detector, has also found out that there are two villages called Chmielowa: one on the northern side of the Dniester River and the other on the opposite bank. Previously he'd asked me, through Alina, which Chmielowa I was referring to: the one in the Tarnopol district or the one in the Ivano-Frankivsk district. As I'd driven through Ivano-Frankivsk on an earlier trip, I automatically said 'Chmielowa Ivano-Frankivsk'. But this turns out to be wrong, and we find ourselves being directed by Google Maps to Chmielowa on the other side of the river. I feel embarrassed about my mistake and Alina feels uncomfortable as she has not met Taras in person: he is driving in a separate vehicle. The expedition seems to be off to a bad start. Alina bites the bullet and phones Taras to tell him. I feel very relieved when she reports back that he just laughed and said he would head to the correct side of the river.

After a long, bumpy drive along potholed roads, we eventually arrive at 'our' Chmielowa at about lunchtime on an overcast Monday, an hour later than scheduled. The mild autumnal air greets us, and the rich earthy odours embrace us. Strangely, I feel that I have come home.

As I get out of the Land Cruiser, I ask Alina to approach the Ukrainian-speaking Taras so that I can make a deal with him in case we find anything. 'No, now is not the right time,' she responds. I never did get round to cutting a deal with Taras, an omission I was later to regret.

We begin a relaxed reconnoitre of the terrain, but I am immediately disorientated: the place has become completely overgrown with bushes and small trees since I was last here some ten years before. And the old memory box is perhaps not what it used to be. The dilapidated stone barn is still there, but the granary has either been restored or completely removed. I am not even sure if what is standing there is in fact the old granary.

I lead the group down towards the river, where I recollect having seen the foundations of the old manor house. But we find nothing. Thorny rosehip bushes have invaded what was previously ground cover and grass. I seem to recollect that, from the manor house, my forebears would have had a view of the river that flows idly below – the view that is depicted in many family photographs. But it turns out I am wrong. We cannot find any sign of the foundations of the house, which were so easy to spot the last time I was here. It is vital that we do so, as the foundation of the yard wall around the main house will be our base point, where my father's dotted line starts on his map. I feel not only deflated but somewhat embarrassed that I have brought this motley crew all this way. Maybe I am imagining it, but I think I overhear Taras mumbling something in Ukrainian about 'romantic foreigners'.

I feel an immediate connection with the affable, silver-haired Taras, but he remains enigmatic. Like me, he is a retired academic. His speciality was medieval archaeology. Communication is difficult: Taras does not speak any English and his Polish is poor; he is fluent in Ukrainian and Russian, but seems keener to talk to Layla, which they manage animatedly by means of Google Translate. I warm to him; he is mild-mannered and seems willing to communicate. We stroll towards the Dniester River valley, surveying the terrain as we go along. During my father's time, this was a cultivated vegetable field; during the communist era cultivation continued, but the area is now covered with grass and low bush.

As we amble along towards the river, Taras tells us in broken Polish that searching for World War II artefacts is a common practice, attracting many hobbyists and amateurs. He mentions that his own speciality is medieval archaeology, for which he has a permit. With some horror it dawns on me that my 'qualified expert' may not have a permit for this particular activity after all. My consternation is worsened when he informs me that Ukraine has enacted a law expropriating all pre-World War II artefacts and making the search for such objects illegal. A shiver goes down my back. I could end up in trouble. And what about Layla?

I wish that I had consulted a few legal colleagues back in South Africa. I ponder whether we should just take a cursory look and leave before an alarm is raised. But then it occurs to me once again that the likelihood of finding anything is remote and I should press on. Such an opportunity is never likely to arise again: the combination of a local expert with a metal detector; my enthusiastic niece; and Alina who speaks Ukrainian and has her own transport. And, in the end, this is my family heritage, and I am carrying out my duty to my beloved father.

As we continue to traipse through the fields, Taras goes on to explain that there are varying classes of specialisation in what he calls 'black archaeology': some deal in World War II artefacts, others in eighteenth- and nineteenth-century relics. It becomes apparent to me that different metal detectors are required for different classes of objects from different eras, made of different substances, and occurring at different depths. I note that the metal detector Taras is carrying is similar to those that hobbyists use on Cape Town beaches to find lost valuables. I frown, as the treasure we are looking for is likely to be buried a metre or more deep. I recollect a conversation many years previously with my geologist friend Clinton, who said that certain metal detectors can sense an object a few metres deep. Taras's instrument, however, does not appear to be one of those. Again, I regret that I have not done my homework thoroughly enough.

We reach the edge of the field and gaze at the forested slope with the river meandering far below us. It is already early afternoon, and we have allocated two, at a stretch three, days for the search – the most important project of my life. Alina must be back in Cracow by the weekend. It is vital that we locate the foundations of the manor house, the starting point on my father's map. In his instructions he wrote: 'On the left side of the pencil drawn map you will see the broken line going from the stone wall towards the forest (oaks)...' My stomach churns at my inability to find this point, and I feel disoriented and anxious. But at Taras's suggestion we make our way down the slope towards the forest to carry out some preliminary exploration with the metal detector. It bleeps a few times, but these turn out to be false alarms. I become even more despondent.

I say a prayer to my ancestors. I won't fail them; I will forge on; I will do my best. I recollect my father often saying, 'If you can't do a job properly, don't do it at all.' For some odd reason, an old song by

Trini Lopez from my teenage years comes into my head: 'Do what you do do well, boy; do what you do do well...' I have not done well. The first day of the search has been disappointing, to say the least.

By now it is late afternoon, and the sky is darkening. We give up our search and Alina drives us to a resort hotel near Zaleszczyki, the market town where my father took his vegetables to sell. The resort is surrounded by a pine forest, and abandoned boats are bobbing on an artificial lake, the summer tourists having departed. Taras arrives in his own vehicle. I feel disheartened and flat. We gather around solid wooden tables in the hotel dining room and bar area; the TV is blaring with flashes of women jiggling their hips. Using my iPad, Taras googles pre-World War II maps of the area, hoping to find details of the layout of the manor house. We have some limited success: he finds a map that appears to depict the farm, but the image consists of mere speckles. There seems to be little chance of finding a clear indicator. Taras suggests that we talk to the local villagers, perhaps the history teacher, who may help us to orientate ourselves on the land.

During dinner, I can't help noticing a nearby table where half a dozen rowdy men are celebrating some occasion. As we come to the end of our meal, one of them comes across and hugs Taras like a long-lost friend. It turns out that he was a student of Taras while the latter was teaching heritage law at the local police college. The man slurringly sings Taras's praises, telling us what a good man and teacher he was. When we ask for the bill, it turns out that Taras's former student has paid for our bottle of wine. Taras tells us later that this man is now the deputy chief of police in the area – which is reassuring for me in case we run into any trouble.

The next morning we return to the village and head to the local school to see if anyone there can tell us about the history of the surrounding area. But because it is a small school, there is no history teacher. Instead, we are directed to the principal's office and are ushered into a small, cluttered room. The principal is somewhat taken aback: not only is it clear that visitors are few and far between around here, but people 'from Africa' have now arrived. Initially he seems defensive and uncooperative, saying that there is no dedicated history of the village area, and in any event he has only been there for the past ten years. And if I correctly understand Marek, our translator, the principal has never heard of the Glazewskis.

Then he begins to listen intently to Taras, gradually perking up and suggesting that we talk to some old people in the village. He leads us down the road and accosts an elderly woman just leaving her house. We engage her in conversation and she suggests talking to her friend, whom she summons just as she is about to go indoors. The elderly friend comes out in what appear to be her gardening clothes, and bashfully says that she is not dressed to talk to strangers. Nevertheless, we engage the two women in conversation, and they tell us about the 'Polish hill' where the landlord used to live. The name Glazewski clearly strikes a chord, and to the somewhat awed audience I announce that I am 'the grandson from Africa'.

Other curious passers-by join us as we stroll down the road, past quaint cottages with abundant gardens. A lost-looking, unshaven man in a shabby white shirt and grey suit jacket joins the fast-growing throng. I think of the Pied Piper. All seem to agree that we should go to *Pani* Paulina's house: she will remember. Along the way I am offered a handful of walnuts by an elderly lady with whom I communicate in broken Polish. Someone mentions that my grandfather was 'a good man' and repeats the story of how the peasants saved him from death at the hands of the Russians.

We eventually reach *Pani* Paulina's house and Taras tells her our business. We make no mention of the treasure but simply say we are trying to locate the old buildings on the farm. The sprightly lady is 92 years old, wears a brown headscarf, a long charcoal skirt to her shins, and out-of-place grey Crocs over long black stockings. She certainly remembers *Pan* Glazewski, the 'Polish landlord on the hill' – in fact, her late sister had worked in my grandfather's kitchen. I am touched to hear that she kept a photograph of him on her mantelpiece – how I wish I could see it. The school principal tells us he must get back to his duties and bids us farewell. Taras persuades *Pani* Paulina to come up the hill to the farm and show us around. Together with her, the man in the shabby suit jacket hops uninvited into Taras's vehicle as we set off to drive the 300 metres or so up the hill, while the others walk. On arrival, the man in the shabby jacket says he will show us where the house was. *Pani* Paulina says in Polish, 'Don't listen to him; he knows nothing.'

While Taras, Alina and I wander around the farm with *Pani* Paulina, the shabby man makes a beeline through the overgrown shrubs and bushes, followed by Layla. She comes back after five minutes, triumphantly crying out that she has found the cellar. Layla asks for my cell phone to take pictures of its interior. After surveying the farm with the sprightly *Pani* Paulina, Taras offers her a lift back down the hill, but she cheerfully refuses and heads down on foot in her flowing dark-coloured attire.

Having found the cellar, the key to locating the original house, Layla and Taras take the lead in searching for the foundations of the house. The two revisit the map yet again when – voila! – something is set off in Layla's mind. She finds remnants of the yard wall adjoining the original house that serves as the base point for the dotted line on my father's map leading towards where the treasure is buried.

It is now mid-afternoon. We follow the imaginary line to the forest and carry out another search. The metal detector bleeps a few times, but these turn out to be false alarms. We leave Chmielowa in the late afternoon and drive back to the resort. Again, I feel somewhat deflated and dispirited. But at least I have tried. Layla, noticing my flagging spirits, says good-heartedly, 'At least now, perhaps, you can let it go, and not hold on to it after all these years.' Not for the first time the thought crosses my mind that, in all probability, the peasants who worked on the farm and in the household would have noticed the missing silver, put two and two together, and dug it up.

The search is over – at least for now. I've put myself in Alina's hands. She has booked a chalet for the next two nights in the Carpathians, a few hours' drive further south. The following morning, we thank and say goodbye to Taras, who is due to drive home to Ivano-Frankivsk. But there is something lingering in the air. It does not feel like a final goodbye to me. Taras mentions that he will contact a friend who has a better metal detector.

As a diversion, we head back to Zaleszczyki. Alina is now keen to show us what turns out to be a picturesque and historic town. Unbeknown to me, she has arranged a walking tour. Our guide is Arkady, who provides a fascinating account of the town, reeling off famous names of leading people who visited over the centuries, including Stanisław Poniatowski, King of Poland and Grand Duke of Lithuania during Poland's heyday in the eighteenth century.

The town is set in a sunken horseshoe, along the banks of the Dniester, which Arkady shows us from a viewing site. At one stage in the twentieth century the Dniester formed the border between Poland and Romania before boundaries were redrawn at the end of World War II. Arkady talks about the history of the imposing bridge that straddles the river. I imagine that this was where my parents and uncles had crossed into Romania when fleeing Poland. (However, once I am back in South Africa my father's mini-memoir reminds me that they crossed at a place nearer to Chmielowa.)

That afternoon, we journey on to the Carpathians. In the car we speculate about returning to continue our search, though generally we avoid talking about what was to me a great disappointment. I feign enjoyment, but deep down I feel a failure. I have let my late father down; I did not prepare thoroughly enough. I allowed Alina to arrange the journey on her terms. I should have negotiated with her that we stay there longer. As far as she is concerned, 'we are having a great road trip'. But I feel remorseful. A lifelong ambition has come to naught and has slipped from my grasp. Although the odds were against me, I feel that I did not try hard enough, even if the chances of finding the buried family silver are minimal.

Now, I am looking forward to what I imagine to be the majestic and imposing Carpathian mountains. But once again I am disappointed: they are nothing in comparison with the mountains of the Western Cape. I am drawn to an imposing signboard indicating a Unesco World Heritage Site: the waterfall nearby. But on scrambling down the path, following the others, I am again disappointed. I see no reason why this small waterfall or large rapid should be designated as a world heritage site. In South Africa one would walk by it and hardly notice it. That evening, Layla, Alina and Marek enjoy a hot-spring bath, while I lie on my bed, examining the ceiling.

It is Thursday morning. We could spend another night in the Carpathians, as we are scheduled to be back in Alina's Lviv flat only on Friday night and to depart for Cracow at the latest on Saturday morning. Alina announces matter-of-factly over coffee that Taras had phoned, asking whether I would be happy to pay $100 to his colleague to hire a better metal detector. The route back to Lviv is through Ivano-Frankivsk, where Taras is waiting for a response. I have invested so much already, and half-heartedly agree, although I have lost my enthusiasm.

After a walk, we climb into the Land Cruiser, heading north to Lviv. We discuss options in the car. Alina will not be able to make the detour to Chmielowa, and suggests dropping Layla and me off in Ivano-Frankivsk, and leaving us in the Ukrainian's hands. Marek is enthusiastic to join Layla and me, but his mother sensibly refuses.

I am ambivalent. If we decide on this option, Layla and I will have to find our own way back to Lviv. Moreover, if we do not return to Lviv by Saturday morning, we will miss the comfort of travelling back to Poland in Alina's vehicle. If we decide on a train, we will have to change carriages at the border because of the different gauges in Ukraine and the European Union. I struggle with my replaced knees and severely damaged elbows, and I will have to rely on Layla to help with my bags when changing at the border. Also, we will have to find accommodation in Lviv. I consider the options as I sit in the back of the car, contemplating the implications of my being dropped off with Layla in the middle of Ukraine in the care of a relatively unknown Ukrainian.

Layla seems uncharacteristically quiet regarding the decision, though she later told me that she was silently willing me to have another go but, recognising my anxiety, did not want to push me. I do not feel comfortable with either option. Taking comfort in the knowledge that I have at least tried, should I plunge into the unknown and make one last attempt, take one last risk, even though something terrible could befall us in Ukraine? I am acutely aware that Layla's parents are anxious about their daughter in a faraway, unknown country.

We are halfway to Ivano-Frankivsk when Taras rings again. He says he is looking for a hotel where Layla and I can overnight before travelling to Chmielowa the next day, Friday, and informs us that he now has a better metal detector to hand. The only problem is that Ivano-Frankivsk is hosting the annual Ukrainian dental convention and all the hotels are full. Another reason not to leave the comfort of Alina's Land Cruiser, I think to myself. I am still lukewarm about the idea, when Taras tells Alina that he has met a former student who speaks English and has been to London, and is keen to help. This buoys my spirits.

I know that we are in a needle-in-a-haystack situation. The forest is vast, and my father's map rudimentary. But I tell myself that this is likely to be the last chance I will ever have. I am blessed by the golden opportunity of being accompanied by a local person with a proper metal detector, as well as by my beloved niece, who is keen to go. Although I am tired and disheartened – it has been an intense, stressful week, with four of us cabined in the Land Cruiser for most of the day – I decide to go for it. I do so only because I know I can count on Layla's support and company. Being on my own with Taras would not have worked for me.

CHAPTER 11

Silverware in Sight

IT IS late Thursday afternoon in Ivano-Frankivsk, Taras's home town. Alina has left for Lwów with Marek, though he was keen to stay with Layla and me for the final search. Taras meets us at a hotel where he has managed to find a room despite the dentists' convention. How useful, it crosses my mind, to have all this expertise around if any of us has teeth knocked out.

Taras invites us for a meander in the old city, and I'm pleasantly surprised by its ancient as well as its new architecture; the outer city is ugly in comparison. He then suggests dinner at a busy local restaurant where we are scheduled to meet Vladimir, the 'student' whom Taras had referred to previously. He arrives late, sweating, and very unlike the pale, scrawny archaeological student that I had imagined. Thick-necked and solidly built, he might have played prop for the Ukrainian national rugby team if they'd had one. His English is poor, if not non-existent, and it turns out that he has not studied in London but rather spent time there for some undisclosed reason. I do not warm to him. He later drops us off at the hotel and bids us farewell. Layla tells me that he held her hand longer than necessary.

Early the next morning, Vladimir collects Layla and me at the hotel where we share a twin-bedded room with a bright tomato-coloured bathroom.

'We are going to pick up Taras at his house,' Vladimir announces.

I am surprised to see a tiny, low-slung Opel Astra, as Taras was driving a large station wagon when he turned up in Chmielowa the previous Monday. Now armed with a second 'radar' detector, Taras climbs into the car, and we begin our journey by purchasing provisions at an 'Italian' delicatessen. I am thankful, as I am already lightheaded, breakfast not being available at the hotel because of the dentists' convention. I gulp down a quick cup of coffee and a muffin. It is an estimated two to three hours to Chmielowa, and Vladimir drives like a madman, overtaking lumbering trucks at breakneck speed. At one point he hits a massive pothole and the car comes to a crunching stop. I envisage being stuck in the middle of Ukraine, hoping for some passer-by to get us back to the nearest town. Vladimir gets out, kicks the offending wheel, and thereafter all seems well as we proceed, though still not with any caution.

*

We arrive at Chmielowa in one piece. I am happy to be out of the car, though uneasy about Vladimir. We gather at the manor house's foundations, the remnants of which Layla had discovered the previous Tuesday. From there I gaze wistfully at the vast forest about a hundred metres from what my father had described as a 'cultivated field', but which is now bush and unkempt grass. It is there that we have to descend the slope towards the forest.

We set off across the field. Taras and Layla lead the way, having taken a rough estimate of the direction from the foundations to the forest. I assume they are guessing the actual location of the dotted line on my father's map – but, as Layla later informed me, she used her phone compass to take the angle from the foundations of the stone wall down the 'broken line...towards the forest', following my father's instructions.

The team forges ahead. I cautiously trudge along behind, ensuring I don't trip over the tufted grass and shrubs, not wanting to twist my new ankle in any holes. It would be disastrous if I fell and had an internal bleed here in the middle of the Ukrainian countryside, as I have left my blood factor with my luggage at Taras's house, miles away.

The flat terrain eventually becomes a slope slanting towards the thick oak forest below. It becomes steeper, bushier and more wooded the further we go. While descending, I realise that my hand is bleeding from a thornbush in my path. Not good for a haemophiliac. I wrap my handkerchief around the bleeding wound. Layla looks back anxiously, and I signal a thumbs-up with my other hand.

I recollect my father's words: 'Where the forest starts…' But where would the forest have started eighty years ago? Over all these intervening years, has it encroached up the slope or possibly receded downwards? Layla is adamant that we should go further down to find the old-growth forest. I try to put myself in my father's shoes as he and his brothers were planning their hasty departure.

The slope gets steeper and the trees thicker. I sit down on the dank leaf-covered earth and say a little 'help me' prayer to my father and grandfather. I meditate on the fact that for decades I have been preparing consciously and subconsciously for this moment. I'd arranged my flat in Cracow as a base camp, engineered my meeting with the Polish-Ukrainian Alina, and have the delight of the company of my youngest niece. Appropriately, Layla is my father's youngest grandchild, who will carry this adventure forward to future generations, whatever may happen. I gradually feel less anxious and more content. If we don't find anything, at least I have given my father's directive a good try.

I return from my reverie and am pleased to see that Taras has started an exploratory probe where the new growth begins, where the trees are not more than ten metres tall. But my stomach gnaws at the fact that I have not struck a deal with him. Should I offer him half if we do find the treasure? And a few dollars if we do not? Layla returns to ask me if I am okay. A chirping robin pops up on the branch of a small tree nearby. 'Could that be grandfather Gustaw giving us a sign?' asks Layla, pointing at the bird.

It occurs to me that the two men with metal detectors are too far down. My father would have simply wanted to be out of sight of any villagers or workers, who would have been on the higher ground above. I feel he would not have gone much further than where we find ourselves. After all, we are now down the slope and out of sight of the homestead and field above.

Taras, armed with his new rectangular 'radar' metal detector, sensibly announces that he will look twenty metres on either side of the imaginary line, starting on the left. Vladimir seems to be running around aimlessly, trying random spots with the original metal detector. I'm reminded of searchers on the beaches in the fading light of Cape Town summers after the tourists have left. I try to imagine what my father and his brothers would have done here all those years ago. One thing is certain – they'd have been in a hurry.

After about fifteen minutes, Taras's metal detector bleeps. It sounds like a child's annoying toy and has a deeper sound than the round metal detector that Layla and Vladimir vie for. I suck in my breath. Could it be? Taras calls Vladimir over, and tells him to try his round detector. It turns out to be a false alarm. About ten minutes later, there is another bleep. We dig, but it's another false alarm: an old nail or something similar. My hopes fade. We are seemingly trying the impossible.

After twenty minutes or so, Taras signals that he'll try on the other side of the imaginary line. I motion him to come up the slope, nearer to where I've been sitting, where I imagine the brothers had dug the hole. And amazingly, within five minutes, there's a resounding bleep. Taras calls Vladimir to bring the other metal detector, but Layla now has it and there's a bit of an altercation as to who will take it to Taras.

The four of us gather around the hotspot. My eyes are riveted, focused on the fallen leaves, willing them to pierce the secrets below.

Vladimir's metal detector continues to produce promising bleeping sounds. He cautions, 'Maybe bomb…', in his Ukrainian accent. I take a step back. There were two world wars that took place here, after all, and the area is popular with 'black archaeologists' searching for old war relics and other artefacts. But the bleep seems to indicate nothing more than an old tin.

Still, Taras urges Vladmir to get to work, and the latter grabs the spade. Her begins to dig furiously, and the black loam yields. He is only about a foot deep when a dull but distinctive *clank* is heard. It is the unmistakable sound of metal. A low 'ah' emerges from deep within Layla. Taras instantly pulls a metal probe from his carry-bag and plunges it into the soft black earth. Could this be it? He slowly removes a layer of leaves, then soil, doing so layer by layer. Silver specks appear in the black earth, growing larger as he works. He motions to Vladimir, who eagerly takes over.

I see the glint of a metal object. I gasp. Layla urges Vladimir to use the spade more slowly, more gently, then she puts her hands into the freshly dug hole and tries to ease the object out. 'Can it be?' I cry in a hushed tone. Layla tries to temper my mounting hope and excitement, warning me, 'It may not be a Glazewski thing.' She glances back at me as a brass candlestick appears. It has been damaged by the aggressive digging. She places it in my outstretched hand. Taras then takes over, probing gingerly in the soft damp soil. Layla and Vladimir jockey for the second spade, taking turns in removing the earth – Layla gently, and Vladimir less so. I watch intently, my chest pounding as I fumble for my – thankfully – fully charged cell phone. I begin to film the process of unearthing what turns out to be my family's long-buried treasure.

Next appears another candlestick, this time silver, the second of well over a dozen that will eventually appear. The gleaming colour contrasts with the dark earth. Then Layla hands me a spoon wrapped in yellowing newspaper; the bone handle has decomposed and is no longer there. I marvel at the fact that the newspaper is seemingly preserved. The banner states *Gazeta Polska*. The print is still clearly visible and readable, but it crumbles as soon as I finger it. I feel choked up and am crying as I hug Layla. 'We've done it!' I gasp. 'You must find our silver and my hunting guns' was the last sentence of my father's typed instructions. I'd never really believed it was possible, though something deep inside me always said I should try. A lifelong dream has been achieved.

Layla is now at knee height in the hole, and she continues to remove the black soil, clearly at home because of her landscaping experience. She uncovers a silver goblet and a candelabrum, and then hands me a square silver box. I open it gently with trembling hands. Inside I find a small silver milk jug and an even smaller, seemingly ebony-encased jewel case, containing some trinkets and a rose crucifix encrusted with amethyst. I feel a strange sensation in the pit of my stomach. Layla remarks that these items were my mother's and would have been touched by her eighty years before. And now, here I am, fingering them eighty years later. My mother would have hurriedly packed these items and placed them carefully in a bag that has seemingly perished with time. My father would have carried it across the field, down the slope, to be quickly buried along with the family silver and his hunting guns. All this buried emotion is uncovered by me, eighty years later.

Layla and Vladimir carry on digging, taking turns: Layla gently and methodically; Vladimir frenzied, like an excited boy, displaying no archaeological delicacy at all. I am astounded at the amount and variety of silverware that is revealed: dozens of silver candlesticks, coffee cups and saucers, cutlery and more. The wooden cutlery boxes have rotted, allowing Layla to scoop up handfuls of teaspoons, spoons, forks and knives, whose bone handles have perished. I marvel at the family crests, some with the Glazewski insignia, though the predominant engraving is 'AR' – the initials of my paternal grandmother,

Adela Romer, who died of the Spanish flu after World War I. She must have brought these into the family as her dowry. Coins and medallions also appear. Some seem to come from Roman times, others are inscribed in Arabic, while yet others are dated in the 1700s or earlier.

I run my hands over some of the pieces. Then Layla delicately presents me with a christening spoon. I see my father's name engraved on it: Gustaw. Elated, I immediately put the spoon in my shirt pocket. If there is one object I am going to smuggle home, it is this. In a sense, I am satisfied with just that one item. But then a feeling of possessiveness washes over me as I look at the many other objects that have been retrieved from their grave.

Vladimir, who is kneeling in the hole, excitedly exclaims, 'Look, from *Dziadzio*!' With boyish delight, he holds up a gleaming silver goblet. 'This is one hundred dollars,' he says triumphantly. But as more and more silverware is uncovered, I sense a change of atmosphere. The by now heavily perspiring Vladimir mutters to Taras, in Ukrainian, 'This belongs to Ukraine – no compensation.'

In my excited, emotional state, I sweep aside any thought that what we are doing may be unlawful. I clench my teeth, thinking, 'This is ours. Not only my father's, but the property of preceding generations. It has my family crest on it.' The uneasiness in the pit of my stomach melts away as further items are uncovered. They join the growing pile of silver objects that Layla and Vladimir are handing to Taras from the hole. Taras, in turn, flings them into his fast-filling carrier bag while I, fumbling in my excitement, take pictures and videos on my cell phone.

'Talabans,' I hear Vladimir exclaim as he grasps one of the many coins and holds it up between his fingers. Later I was to learn that I heard incorrectly and that he was referring to thalers, one of the large silver coins minted in the Holy Roman Empire and the Habsburg monarchy in the early modern era. I had no idea that anyone in the family was a coin collector.

Some of the coins turn out to be medallions – one is inscribed 'A Glazewski Mission Agricole 1925'. I recollect my father saying that grandfather Adam was involved in local land affairs, but I'd not realised that he, like my father, had agricultural interests, and also had close ties with France. It now makes sense to me that my father and brothers had French tutors and a French governess, and that *Strij Kot* ended up in France. As I ruminate, I am astounded at how much is still being unearthed – there's clearly an abundance of silver objects.

I see Taras and Vladimir having a surreptitious consultation on the side and assume that they are concerned about the village women we'd previously noticed picking berries. Perhaps the women are spying on us and will report us to the local police.

We have come totally unprepared for the huge hoard, which includes a large silver tray. Taras roughly throws the items into the over-full shoulder bag that he had brought for his archaeological equipment. He suggests that Layla and Vladimir take it up to the car and empty it there. I suggest they pose as boyfriend and girlfriend to avoid suspicion. This elicits a leer from Vladimir and a shudder from Layla. Nevertheless, she accompanies him reluctantly, posing as his partner, as if they have been in the forest for a picnic. They dump the articles in the boot and return for the next load. When we eventually weigh the entire haul, it comes to over 30 kilograms.

After about two elated hours, there are no more silver items, but we strike a large metallic object: this is one of two 'hunting guns' that my father referred to in his instructions. They are completely rusted, though. In addition, there are some rusted ceremonial sabres and long-bladed knives, which my father never mentioned. One ceremonial sabre in particular grabs my attention as it has a jewel-encrusted handle. I learn later that this was given to older sons by their father to carry on the warrior tradition. I have found a sabre that has, in a very real sense, been passed on to me by my father. I regret not having a son of my own to pass it on to.

The diggers at last hit bedrock and do a last metal detector sweep. We throw the rusty guns back in the hole; it is not worth trying to restore them. I look wistfully at the two rusty sabres, particularly the one with an ornate handle, and decide to take them, even though I do not want to be found with them in Ukraine. We throw some of the black earth over the items and make a hasty departure back up the slope.

*

Taras and Vladimir have already made their way to the car. As I follow Layla up the slope, she pauses and tells me that she has a mental image of the four brothers hastily going down the slope with bags of silver in 1939. Now in 2019, almost to the day, we are doing the opposite, carrying the same silver up the slope.

I am elated. Taras is packing the car and I sense that he is nervous and wants to get going. I insist on some last-minute photographs of myself with the two Ukrainians and Layla against the backdrop of the 'cultivated field', the river, and the forest in the distance. Fortunately, there is just enough battery charge on my cell phone.

As we leave Chmielowa, I wonder if this may be my last visit. We drive through the village, seemingly unnoticed, cross the Dniester River, and stop at an abandoned roadside picnic area where we hungrily devour the provisions we've brought with us.

I have found 'our' silver and 'my' hunting guns, and the significance of it all continues to grow on me as the weeks and months pass. I have fulfilled my father's directive and a lifelong dream.

*

The haul is in the boot of Vladimir's car. The first step is to return to Ivano-Frankivsk, where both Taras and Vladimir live. The autumn sun is now setting. En route to that town I ponder the immediate question: how to get all this back to Lviv, where we are scheduled to rendezvous with Alina the next day and return with her to Cracow.

And what to do with it then? We are disinclined to take it across the border. If it was just grandmother's tea set, maybe, but a 30-kilogram haul of silver with over 150 coins and medallions? Unthinkable!

I muse that I had never really believed we would find the treasure, and in any event never expected how large it would be. I had never decided what to do with it all in the unlikely event that I ever found it. But I do have the silver spoon engraved with my father's name in my shirt pocket.

Layla and I had originally planned to get back to Lviv by bus or train, but this will now be impossible, what with our luggage and two carrier bags crammed with clanking silver. Vladimir tells us that, since he often travelled to Poland via Lviv, he can drop us off at Alina's flat with the haul after delivering Taras to Ivano-Frankivsk. I gratefully accept the offer – a huge weight has seemingly been lifted off my shoulders.

It is dusk by the time we get back to Taras's home. We take the bags stealthily inside and spread the loot on the carpet. I snap some pictures and send them to Louise in South Africa, the first person I notify of our success. I think about how to compensate Taras and his helper, Vladimir. While I am asking Taras whether he'd be happy with the magnificent encrusted goblet, Vladimir has already set aside several silver coffee cups and saucers for himself, as well as a couple of other items. I feel tension rising in me. Layla says that they deserve this for all their work. Vladimir tells me that Taras would like a beautiful candelabrum, which I had earmarked for a cousin in Paris. I am suddenly angry with Vladimir, but I calmly remove two of the six silver coffee cups and saucers from the pile that Vladimir has amassed for himself. The remark I'd first made years ago, that I would be happy with just a teaspoon, has gone out of the window. Layla calms the situation by pointing out that, but for the two Ukrainians, we'd never have found anything. True, but we would have done so without Vladimir. I shrug, the tension dissipates, and both men seem happy.

Taras's wife offers us a delicious meal of chicken broth, and I hungrily take up the offer although I am keen to get back to Lviv. We gather all the silver in a suitcase and several bags that Taras provides. I regretfully decide to leave the two rusty sabres with Taras. They are too bulky and seemingly dangerous to be caught with. After bidding a warm farewell to Taras and his wife, we leave in Vladimir's Opel Astra. It is about two and a half hours' drive to Lviv.

Vladimir drives fast and recklessly, but we chat on the way. He cheerfully informs us that he is a part-time policeman and that he monitors the illegal movement of pharmaceutical products across the Polish–Ukrainian border – a particularly well-monitored border, as it is an entry point into the European Union. I gulp.

At last we reach the familiar cobblestoned streets of Lviv. We park outside Alina's flat, unload the silver, and Marek comes to assist us. Vladimir does not come upstairs. I bid him farewell and tell him that we intend to travel by car to Poland with Alina the next day. His last words to me are: 'If you have any trouble at the border, do not hesitate to phone me.' He is clearly well connected and, so it occurs to me later, he now also knows the location of Alina's flat.

*

We enter the flat in high spirits. Alina is playing Queen's 'We Are the Champions' at full blast and has cracked open a bottle of champagne. I am exhausted but elated. Once again, we lay out a large number of items on the floor, with some prize pieces on the kitchen table, including the coins and medallions. I notice a distinctive lead-coloured cross with an embossed gold medal at the centre. It is engraved 'Virtuti Militari 1792', words that Marek excitedly recognises from his history classes, and so he feverishly carries out a Google search. It reveals that 150 or so of these have been awarded throughout Polish history for valour during significant events, usually battles. I speculate that it may have been awarded to my great-grandfather Ignacy, who, according to my father, was involved in the Polish uprising against Russia in 1830–1831. After some deliberation about what to do with the medallion, I admit to myself that if I take it back to South Africa, it will probably lie around in a bottom drawer. I decide to give it to Marek, who seems extremely touched by the gesture. I am pleased it will remain in Poland, where it belongs. I would later discover through a Google search that the rare Virtuti Militari was in fact awarded to Franciszek Paszkowski, whose descendant Leon is buried alongside my grandfather.

Alina has to get back to her family in Cracow, and so, next morning, we wake early. Layla hastily rearranges the items on the carpet, grouping them into rough categories: candlesticks; solid silver soup ladles; small silver milk jugs; cutlery, including forks, spoons and teaspoons. Alina reminds us that the flat must be thoroughly cleaned before we leave at eleven, as her guests are due to arrive in the afternoon. There is no time to make a thorough inventory, but Layla takes some pictures of the hoard spread out over the carpet. We hurriedly pack the items into two large tog bags, along with the 150 or so coins. They will all be left with Alina's friend Roman. Although he is a complete stranger to me, I have to entrust him with the bulk of the silver. I don't have much choice in the matter, as I know no one in Lviv and it cannot remain in Alina's flat, where guests constantly come and go. We decide, however, to each pack some items in our luggage, amounting to about one kilogram. This includes the silver cross that I have already given to Marek. The rest will remain with Roman in Lviv, including a number of precious coins and medallions.

We pack the vehicle and are nervous throughout the two-hour trip to the Ukrainian–Polish border. As Vladimir had announced, this border is particularly strictly policed, as it marks the divide between EU and non-EU countries – including Ukraine. I try to deflate the tension by asking my companions whether they can identify at least half of the countries of Africa. Alina's son demonstrates his general knowledge by starting to rattle off the 50 states of the US, but I steer him back on track and he manages with ease, with a little help from Layla and his mother.

Some two hours later, we approach the border and tension mounts again in the car. We are acutely aware that if the items in our luggage (and some coins in a canvas pouch around my neck) come to the attention of the border police, we may face some difficult questioning – even though what we have belongs rightfully to my family. Alina has described how the customs officials are trained to look you in the eye, and so we'd be well advised not to avert our eyes, and to return their gaze.

We stop behind a line of cars and wait patiently but nervously. Layla is in the back with Marek and tries to break the tension by checking my Ukrainian road map and reciting the names of all the towns we have travelled through over the past week. An official comes to the car and beckons Alina, who is driving, to come to the office with all our passports. This is standard procedure. By now I have a Polish passport, and I am relieved I do not have to worry about my South African passport attracting extra scrutiny.

I note that the travellers in front of us are asked to remove all their luggage and place it on a concrete bench alongside the line of cars. The brown-uniformed Ukrainian officials poke around their goods thoroughly. If they do the same to us, we are doomed, and I wonder how it will all end up. Layla suggests praying to Gustaw, which we do. (Afterwards she told me that she and her parents in Rheenendal had texted each other throughout the ordeal.) The prayers evidently worked because as soon as the car in front had repacked its boot, we are waved through and proceed to the Polish border guard a hundred metres away. The biggest hurdle is over, and I heave a huge sigh.

A similar procedure is carried out at the Polish border post. Alina is summoned to the passport office by a stern blonde customs official who takes all our passports. After an uncomfortable fifteen minutes in the car, Alina returns in conversation with the female official.

'So he doesn't speak Polish?' she says in that language.

I realise that the computer in the passport office would have shown that I travel on two passports. While I am mulling this over in the passenger seat, the official walks to the rear and orders Alina to open the boot. She casts her piercing blue eyes over our luggage.

I hear her ask in Polish, 'Who owns the green case?'

I immediately regret having bought the striking green suitcase.

'*Pan* Jan,' answers Alina, and summons me from the back seat.

My heart is thumping, and I immediately engage the official: 'Mowiem trochę po Polsku' (I speak a little Polish). I see her eyes light up and a little smile developing at the corners of her mouth. Poles all seem to love my foreign, old-fashioned accent.

But then she barks: 'Is this your suitcase?'

I nod.

'Open up!' she orders.

My heart is sinking as I unzip the bag. But I engage her in the best Polish I can muster.

'Yes, I live in South Africa. In Cape Town, in fact. A beautiful city. Have you heard of Table Mountain? You should visit sometime.'

'Hm,' she says distractedly, 'isn't there a lot of crime there?'

'No,' I reply, 'only in certain areas.'

'Ah, okay,' she concludes the conversation, and takes a step away. I zip my case, noting that five centimetres below my thick woollen jersey was a solid silver soup ladle and several other items. I get back into the car, my legs wobbling like a stranded jellyfish on a Cape beach.

*

We arrive back in Cracow on Saturday evening exactly a week after we left, but it feels as if a lifetime has passed since starting out. As the Sunday morning light begins to filter through the bedroom curtains of my flat, I vividly feel my late father's presence. He is no doubt glowing with pride in whatever spiritual realm he finds himself in. With a start, I remind myself that *Tatuś* is no longer with us. But I feel close to him. I have fulfilled his instructions and reclaimed the family heritage. I wish I had probed my father for details of the silver. He never really spoke about the treasure, so I was not prepared for such a hoard dating back hundreds of years and many generations. And my father had never mentioned the sabres or the Virtuti Militari medallion, the Polish equivalent of the Victoria Cross.

The first thing I do that Sunday morning is joyfully notify those whom I have not yet informed of our success: family, friends, and my French cousins. Their father had assisted mine in burying the trove, and had also left them a map. I am delighted to hear from my cousin Adam's adult daughter Anna, whom I have met only once. She is enthralled, and recounts how she had heard the story of the buried treasure at her own grandfather's knee. I delight in reinforcing these distant, even remote, family connections.

Some friends and family members express disbelief, but all are happily surprised. Layla arranges the photographs and videos taken on my iPhone and makes a small movie clip. I painstakingly sort the dozen or so coins and medallions we'd smuggled out along with a few items of silver. Although I am now in Poland, it is imperative for me to devise a plan to get the bulk of the haul out of Ukraine at some later time, at least to Poland. But how?

On Monday morning, two days after leaving Lviv, my phone gives a familiar bleep. I expect another congratulatory text. But instead I read: 'Hi, me and Taras have found with you a lot of gold and silver. All that we found belongs to Ukraine, and we had no right to take it, we committed a crime, it is a big risk if we have problems, then we have nothing to do with what we found! Therefore, you must share silver and gold coins with us. Except for family relics. I give you two days you have to split the coins or pay 2 000 dollars for help and risk.'

It is from Vladimir. My heart freezes. This is so unexpected, as I had given the two Ukrainians some of the prize pieces of silver: the candelabrum, goblet, coffee cups and more. Taras came across as an easy-going and affable academic archaeologist, but he has seemingly done an about-face and is under Vladimir's influence. Vladimir, whom Taras had recruited, has poisoned the waters. We felt we had left Taras's house on amicable terms, after a hearty dinner prepared by his wife, with hugs and promises to return. It's a relief to me that Layla and I are booked on a homeward flight back to South Africa in a few days' time. We can avoid any unpleasantness by just leaving.

But then the chilling realisation hits me: Vladimir knows where Alina's flat is located in Lviv. He could easily trace her to Cracow and may even cause harm to her or her children. I think of movies I have watched about the violent Ukrainian mafia, and take small comfort in the fact that neither Alina nor her son was involved on the day of the actual find. Yet they might themselves be dragged into the matter. I pondered about what role Taras might be playing in this new and opportunistic development. On the one hand, I'd made a big mistake in not coming to an agreement with Taras at the outset of our expedition before Vladimir came into the picture; on the other hand, my original idea of a deal had been that I would give him half of what we found. In retrospect, I would not have been happy with that. I did give him two prize pieces – a goblet and a beautiful candelabrum. He and his wife seemed happy and content when they saw us off in Vladimir's car, carrying the rest of the heirlooms in its boot.

I hesitate about notifying Alina, but it is the right thing to do. So, I forward the text to her. I also want to talk to Taras, but because of the language barrier I hope that Alina can speak to him and hammer some sense into him. I am adamant that I will not deal with Vladimir, as I had not recruited him. I hope that Taras will have a more even-handed approach.

Alina is occupied with some French tourists who want to hear the inside story about her book. I anxiously wait for her call until evening, when she comes back to me. She is shocked and near hysterical, shouting about the Ukrainian mafia and what they might do to one.

'You sort it out!' she demands. 'They could destroy me.'

On Tuesday Alina phones her husband, who is abroad on a work-related exercise. He advises upgrading the security system at their house. After she tells me this, I try to calm her, suggesting that we do not deal with Vladimir, and that we phone Taras in Ukraine, as it was he who had recruited Vladimir. The problem is that I cannot speak Ukrainian and Alina is adamant that she will not speak to Taras ever again. She firmly states, 'You have to deal with this.' However, she agrees to find an interpreter through whom I can talk to Taras and hopefully get Vladimir off our back.

We have a stressful preliminary meeting – Alina, Layla and I. I acknowledge that both men deserve to be paid something more than they have already received, but I don't want to deal with Vladimir and certainly not meet him, assuming that he comes to Poland. We have visions of handing him cash in the central square and then being followed by Ukrainian mobsters back to my flat. We toy with the possibility of transferring cash, including leaving it at a church that has a drop-off and pick-up facility for foreign travellers. I have a sleepless night.

Next morning, Wednesday, Layla, who is staying in the flat with me, continues to discuss our strategy for the scheduled meeting at two o'clock. She also calls her concerned parents back in South Africa to update them and hear their suggestions. She googles the US dollar price of silver and finds that it is $700 per kilo (well over R10 000). However, we have no indication of the quality or grade of the silver that is being discussed, nor do we have any idea of the value of the coins and medallions. We'd had no opportunity to weigh the silver, but we estimate its weight to be between 20 and 30 kilograms. Alina confirms that she has discussed the highly unusual situation with an interpreter friend, who reluctantly agrees to assist – for a fee, and provided that we do not disclose his name. We duly christen him 'Tomek'. He will come to my flat at two the following afternoon, and I will speak to Taras via Tomek on Viber or WhatsApp.

Adding to my stress is the fact that, an hour before the scheduled arrival of the interpreter, Clinton, one of my best friends, the geologist from university days, arrives in Cracow from Canada for a visit, as arranged months before, to coincide with a conference in Europe. Clinton listens wide-eyed as I explain the drama of the last few days. He needs to rest, he says, and decides not to join us for the meeting with the interpreter.

After a quick lunch, Tomek arrives and we manage to contact Taras in Ukraine by a Viber call. He is a changed man. Before, he was amiable and cooperative; now he sounds bitter and angry. I have a set of prepared notes in front of me, with points that I want to raise. After a few somewhat forced polite introductory remarks, I state my opening condition, that I am prepared to negotiate with him but not with Vladimir. Moreover, I refuse to be blackmailed but am willing to talk about a settlement. I kick off by asking what he wants.

'$3 000 for me and $2 000 for Vladimir,' Taras replies.

I tell him that is not possible, and the haranguing starts.

Much of the negotiation revolves around the weight and monetary value of the silver and the coins. Taras asserts that the silver weighs 50 kilograms; Layla insists it was about 20 (we are on speakerphone). Tomek looks extremely uncomfortable. The point is that none of us knows the weight of the hoard or its current value, and, in any event, the monetary value is not relevant to me: my interest is emotional and sentimental. I am in Cracow, he is in Ivano-Frankivsk, and the silver is in Lviv in the flat of Roman, a stranger to me but a friend of Alina.

On further questioning by Taras, I tell a white lie, namely, that the hoard is in the safekeeping of a connection at the Polish consulate in

Lviv. There is also some discussion about the coins, which he asserts are worth hundreds of dollars. In reality none of us has a clue as to their monetary value – and I get the impression that he doesn't either. The haggling goes back and forth for two hours, covering the same ground. Eventually, we agree that I will pay him $2 000 in total for his work. I emphasise that he must sort out Vladimir from this sum; I refuse to deal with him. It is late afternoon, and I assure Taras that I will transfer the funds first thing tomorrow.

But soon after our Viber conversation I get a text message from Taras: 'Hand over $2 000 cash by 6.00 pm this evening or else. Vladimir is waiting for your call.'

*

The next morning I face the practical problem of transferring $2 000 from my Polish bank account to an account in Ukraine. Taras wants the money at once. He knows that Layla and I are going back to 'Africa' and, rather than giving me his bank account details, he wants a money transfer via his mobile number. After a kilometre-long walk to my bank, I find out that they do not make transfers outside Poland. I have no choice but to withdraw the amount in cash and try sending it through Western Union, which will hopefully facilitate the cash transfer.

The further bad news is that my bank does not have enough foreign currency at this time, so I can only draw 1 000 euros (roughly the equivalent of $1 000 at the time) and I have to schlep another kilometre to another branch for the balance. When I get to the appointed address and after queuing, I am confronted by a scowling woman at the counter. I ask whether I can draw 1 000 euros, and I am rudely dismissed with the words, 'This is not a bank.' She is completely uninterested in assisting me further, and I wander out in confusion. But then I notice from the small print on the sign outside that this is Santander credit bank, and the bank I am looking for is right next door.

Why could the woman not just say so? While in the long queue, I do a Google Maps search for Western Union. To my surprise, it is on the outskirts of town – I would have expected it to be in the central square, where all the tourists hang out.

By now it is mid-morning. This time last week we had just found the silver; it seems so long ago. I have 2 000 euros in my shirt pocket, I am stressed, hot and bothered after much walking, and I decide to take a taxi rather than a tram to the Western Union address I'd googled. The Friday traffic is slow-moving, and I am frustrated to see trams whizzing by in the middle lane. My stress is exacerbated by the fact that my phone bleeps: it is Taras demanding to know, in a mixture of Cyrillic and English, where the money is. 'On the way to the bank,' I text back, hoping he can use Google Translate.

I am mystified when we arrive at the indicated address; we are in an industrial area and there is nothing that resembles a bank, just a bicycle shop and a few modest, office-like buildings. With some trepidation I instruct the Romanian taxi driver to leave me here anyway; then I hesitate, thinking that maybe I should get him to wait while I investigate the bicycle shop. My phone bleeps. Again, it is Taras, but I ignore him this time.

I dismiss the taxi driver, and a friendly bicycle shop attendant informs me that I am not the first person looking for Western Union.

'It is probably a fraud,' he cheerfully adds. He helpfully googles and gives me the address in the central square – where I'd expected it to be.

At least the 2 000 euros are still safe in my shirt pocket. I make my way to the tram stop to return to where I've just come from. On the tram, my phone bleeps again. This time it is Vladimir, who texts: 'What is the problem? Why can't you do what you promised? You're not playing that game.'

I get to the appointed address in the central square, but there is no Western Union sign. I am exasperated, exhausted and anxious. I

183

ask a waiter at a café, 'Where is Western Union?' He shrugs, but his colleague points to a sign right behind us marked 'Kantor' (exchange). I did not imagine that Western Union would have a counter in the Kantor.

As I enter the building, my phone bleeps. Again, it is Vladimir, now becoming more aggressive: 'Do we understand that you are going to Africa? Yan, behave like a man as due to your inappropriate behaviour Alina might suffer.'

I stop in my tracks and read further: 'Vee know you leave for Africa tomorrow morning.'

This text shakes me – they cannot get me or Layla as we will be back in South Africa, but they'd certainly be able to trace Alina. I inform the only woman in the Kantor of my business, and she appears helpful. I am struck by her fine features, and the tortoiseshell glasses she wears. I haul out the wad of euros, but she informs me that they only deal in US dollars. So I exchange the euros for Polish złoty and then back to US dollars. I then proceed to give her Taras's Ukraine phone number and my Polish ID details, which she enters into her computer.

But then I am surprised when she asks me to confirm that I also have a South African passport and refers to my Polish address, which she reads out. 'Big brother knows all about me' is the thought that occurs to me. She continues to punch information into the computer, stares intently at the screen in front of her, but then her demeanour visibly changes. She frowns and shakes her head. 'Not possible,' she says.

'Why?' I ask in a small panic.

'The amount is too high,' she responds.

'Then I will send half.' I am almost pleading now.

She stares at her screen for a minute and again shakes her head. She has now become completely uncommunicative and I imagine that, given the international security networks, I have somehow been blacklisted by Vladimir. And if I'm blacklisted here at the bank, maybe Vladimir has seen to it that I am similarly tagged at the passport control offices at the Ukrainian border should I ever go back. I make my way to my flat, feeling like a fugitive. I am exasperated. Why am I blocked from transferring funds? How am I going to avert disaster?

Layla has gone by bus to visit her half-sister in Budapest for the weekend. I don't want to consult Alina as she is already stressed about this whole affair. On my return to the flat I am relieved to find that Clinton is there, and we can discuss the matter. After much head-scratching, we come up with a plan: if, for whatever reason, my bank account is blocked, there is no reason why Clinton, who has a Canadian passport, should be similarly treated. I will simply give him the cash and he'll transfer the funds. It is already evening, and we can only do this the next day. I wonder if the bank will be open on a Saturday. I am reluctant to go back to the same exchange office, but we discover that there is another branch of Western Union, also in the central square. I then inform Vladimir by text: 'The problem is that Western Union says I can't send my money on my Polish passport. Tomorrow I give the money to my Canadian friend and try to transfer to Taras via him.'

Next morning, Clinton and I head to the central square, dodging the hundreds of tourists who seem to be wandering around aimlessly, licking ice creams. I feel like an internationally wanted criminal. When we arrive at this branch of Western Union we learn the good news that Clinton can send funds to the Ukraine, though there is a daily limit of $1 000. I do the maths and calculate that there is not a huge difference between $1 000 and 1 000 euros. Feeling increasingly like a villain, I slip the euros to Clinton, who in turn hands them to the teller. She does the necessary conversion and sends the funds in Clinton's name. I immediately photograph the proof of payment and send it to Taras. I inform Vladimir that I can only send $1 000 per day, and that the other half will be sent the next day. He responds:

'Why can't the other half be forwarded today? Let Alina in her name pass!' – a demand I understood to mean: 'Send the other half through Alina!' This, of course, I would not do, as Alina has refused to have any dealings with the two of them.

We leave the forex kiosk. Clinton admonishes me for giving him a high-five while the teller's attention was diverted, and for giving his leg a kick to signal that he should change one detail in the form. 'There were cameras behind us in the kiosk,' he hisses as we walk out of the door.

Soon afterwards, I hear from Taras that he has received the first instalment and is looking forward to the balance. I stare almost in disbelief at the message that the transaction has been successful and can start to relax at last. But there is still the question of the second tranche. I am pleasantly surprised to learn from the teller that the branch will be open the next day, as virtually everything, apart from little corner cafés, is closed on a Sunday in Poland so that families can spend time together. On Sunday morning we repeat the same procedure without incident, and again inform Taras. All is done at last, and I can relax.

This has been the most stressful week of my life.

Although it is Sunday, the Rugby World Cup is in full swing. Clinton and I head to the Irish pub in the Rynek to watch South Africa play Japan in the quarter-final, and to drink a beer. It all seems surreal after the events of the week. At half-time, I text Taras. He phones back and acknowledges receipt of the funds. The nightmare, it seems, is over.

*

A week later I return triumphantly to Cape Town, but without my luggage, which has been lost en route. I had distributed the kilo or so of silver which I'd brought from Ukraine between my hand luggage and hold luggage, and am relieved when it arrives intact some

24 hours later.

In my early morning slumbers, a vivid image appears: my father is still alive, and I phone him as soon as I am able to, upon leaving the site of our success. He must be the first to know.

Although we usually conversed in English, my imaginary conversation goes something like this:

'Znalazłem!' (Found it!)

'Co? Niesamowite! (What? Incredible!)

I hear the customary chuckle in the back of his throat. He was not a man given to dramatic displays of emotion, but I know that my news has satisfied him.

I spend the first week of my return compiling a PowerPoint presentation titled 'Silver: Buried September 1939, Found October 2019', which I plan to present to my family over the weekend. The presentation includes photographs and videos of the adventure, as well as some history of the embattled region. This is the first time I can remember my extended family of sisters, nephews and nieces being gathered together in one room, with their spouses. I estimate that there are thirty in the room. A young nephew has brought a video camera, a recently acquired birthday present, to film the presentation, while a niece has connected with her sister in London via Zoom. There is a buzz of excitement in the room. The group is enthralled by my presentation. Relatives who had previously seemed to regard me as a bumbling, absent-minded professor now gaze at me with what seems like open admiration.

Straight after the presentation I unveil the items of silverware and coins that I'd managed to bring back. The group gather round the table, and marvel at the exquisitely worked jewellery box, the cutlery, the candlesticks, coffee cups, coins and medallions, as well as the set of six delicate teaspoons engraved with the letters 'AR'. They look wistfully at the collection. While I am wary of breaking up and distributing the collection among my large family, on an impulse I invite my two older sisters, Wanda and Krysia, to select an item or two. Wanda chooses my mother's trinket box and a ring, while Krysia decides on a small milk jug as well as the christening teaspoon with my father's name engraved on it. I bite my tongue, but I take comfort in the fact that there is an identical breakfast spoon, which I have kept.

A few months later Krysia takes the coveted teaspoon to a framing shop on Main Road in Diep River. She wants it framed in a little wooden box with a velvet cloth background. When she returns ten days later to collect it, she learns that the shop has been robbed and most of the contents have gone. My father's precious christening teaspoon, safely squirrelled underground for eighty years, disappears within two months of its passage to South Africa. I'm angry and distraught and arrange notices for local pawnshops, but to no avail.

I realise I am merely the custodian of the family treasure for future generations, and that it is not only the people in this room who share an entitlement, but also family and relatives in Poland, France and the United States. Certainly, the silver does not belong to me alone. I regret once again that I do not have children, particularly a son, to whom I might pass on some of it. But I feel content in the knowledge at least that these young people in the room will forever hold my father and his family in their memory. The light in the eyes of the younger generation in the room assures me that this will be so.

In subsequent weeks and months, I muse on what I should do with the rest of this large find, assuming I can get it out of Ukraine. Should I give select pieces to specific family members, including the French and Polish cousins? Or would it be more appropriate to keep the pieces in one large display cabinet in a public place or in my flat in Poland, along with the story of how it was buried and recovered?

CHAPTER 12

Dark Clouds, Silver Linings

IN DECEMBER 2019, barely three months after my return to Cape Town, Louise made a proposal that would profoundly affect events relating to the silver. By this time, I had presented numerous talks to family, friends and colleagues about our remarkable feat. These were generally received with acclaim and much amazement, especially since I also displayed the items of silverware as well as the medallions and coins we had managed to recover from Ukraine, though they made up less than a tenth of what still remained in Lviv.

After one of these dinner-party talks, Louise got it into her head that we should return to Ukraine to retrieve the treasure or at least remove it to a more secure location in Lviv. But I was not keen. It was the height of summer in Cape Town; I had invited a friend to accompany me to the traditional New Year cricket test at Newlands, a needle match between South Africa and England. As far as I was concerned, the treasure was safely stowed away with Roman, albeit a stranger, in his cupboard in Ukraine. I felt confident that some plan for retrieving it would emerge in due course. Moreover, I did not have the appetite to head into the middle of the European winter.

But most of all I was frightened. I got it into my head that Vladimir, given his involvement in customs control, would have alerted the Ukrainian and Polish border police. I had sleepless nights imagining that as soon as they scanned my passport, a red flag would come up, and while they might not arrest me then, they would follow our movements around Lviv. Louise and I talked about entering and departing from the country separately so that she would not be implicated and, more importantly, she could sound an alert to the outside world in case I was arrested. Later, Louise told me that she had googled the name and contact details of the South African ambassador to Ukraine, but this did not instil much confidence in me.

Nevertheless, Louise ploughed on with her plans. She discovered that if we flew at midnight on New Year's Eve we could travel at half price. So, we boarded an Austrian Airlines flight in 2019 and took off from Cape Town in the early hours of 2020. Little did I know how fortuitous this decision was – three months later, the whole world would be turned upside down because of the coronavirus lockdowns, making travel impossible. The Cracow flat was our base, and after some debate as to whether it would be wiser to take a day train to Lviv or fly by Ryanair, we decided on the latter option, departing for Lviv on the first Tuesday of 2020 and returning to Cracow the following Saturday.

I had contacted my French cousins in the hope that they could provide some leads and even join us on the mission to recover the treasure from Lviv. Jojo declined the invitation, but Adam, who lives outside Bordeaux, agreed to meet us in Cracow and join us on our adventure, beginning with the Ryanair flight to Lviv. I was looking forward to forging a closer bond with my distant cousin and did not foresee that his presence would in fact prove vital to the whole expedition.

Before departing from South Africa, I contacted my lawyer colleagues and friends to arrange legal back-up in case the worst eventuated. I thought I had hit the jackpot when a friend and partner at a leading commercial law firm referred me to his Oxbridge-educated, Russian-born colleague who was fluent in Ukrainian. But it was December, and he was taking his annual summer holiday and could not be contacted.

In any event, what lawyer would want to defend a nutty law professor who had taken it upon himself to venture twice into the lion's den of Ukraine. All the photos I'd taken of our expedition the previous October were still on my phone. I could, of course, delete this incriminating evidence, but I probably persuaded myself that my technical ineptitude in creating back-ups prevented me from doing so. I remembered hearing a talk by Beatrice Ndlovu, a leading Zimbabwean human rights lawyer, who described the stupidity of two American journalists who had incriminating evidence on their computers. She went to great lengths to secure their release so that they could leave Zimbabwe, but they returned a few months later and were promptly rearrested as they still had the same evidence on their laptops. I was doing something similar; my photo and videos had not been deleted from my phone. I just could not bring myself to do so. But, as things turned out, there was perhaps some hidden hand involved, as the photographs and videos played a key role in my eventual success in getting the treasure out of Ukraine.

Before leaving Cracow for Lviv, we worked on formulating a more concrete plan to retrieve the treasure. I adopted my characteristic shotgun approach, trying any lead I could think of. One of these entailed emailing the Polish ambassador in Kyiv, who was related to a distant cousin, asking if there was any way the embassy could assist in transferring out of Ukraine Polish heritage items that had belonged to my family. Unsurprisingly, he did not reply. I also sought advice from Andrzej Freyman in Canada, who had family connections in Cracow. Our fathers had met in Cairo in the war years and remained friends until their death. Andrzej put me on to an elderly couple in Cracow whose son-in-law, a medical doctor, travelled regularly to Lviv, suggesting that he might carry it out in small quantities each time he journeyed there. On arrival in Cracow, Louise and I immediately visited the couple, but the son-in-law would not even consider the proposition.

FINDING SILVER... AND GOLD

My French cousin Adam had, in the meantime, suggested we contact a French-Polish family friend, Andrzej Jendrzieowicz, who lived in Cracow. He had visited South Africa some years previously and Louise and I had lunched with him at Kirstenbosch Gardens. After Adam arrived in Cracow, we invited Andrzej for soup to discuss several options before our departure to Lviv. He proposed that we use diplomatic means – namely, his Order of Malta membership card – as an excuse for carrying contraband goods across the border. Another suggestion was that we use my health status to get an ambulance to take us back across the border. None of these ideas seemed particularly promising. Andrzej also provided the contact details of one *Pani* Halina, who had been a housekeeper for a Polish countess, and had inherited her employer's palazzo in Lviv. Perhaps we could store the silver hoard there, rather than at some unknown Ukrainian's flat. It turned out that this connection was to prove invaluable – but not in the manner foreseen by Andrzej.

So there we were, the three of us, cousin Adam, Louise and I, arriving on a Ryanair flight at mid-morning on a clear but cold winter's day, 7 January 2020 – which, unbeknown to me, turned out to be Christmas Day in the calendar of the dominant Orthodox Church in Ukraine. I learned this from the taxi driver, who easily understood my rudimentary Polish en route from the airport. Colourful banners lined the cobblestone streets, blocking the road to the George Hotel, and ceremonial pageants were taking place in the city centre. One of four precious days in Lviv had been lost, I thought, as we would not be able to raise anybody on that festive day. We were scheduled to depart again on the following Saturday, and so we had only four short days in the town. We had no definite plan about how to extract the silver from Ukraine, just a bunch of ideas and a few contacts who could possibly help us.

But the three of us were excited to be in this historic city, now dominated by Ukrainians, where numerous ethnic groups had lived for centuries with their various cultural and religious traditions, establishing separate yet interdependent communities within the city – Poles, Jews, Armenians. The first thing I did upon checking in at the fading but once grand George Hotel was to phone Roman, Alina's friend, to whom we had entrusted our 'left luggage', as we discreetly called the treasure. Although it was Christmas Day, he agreed to rendezvous with us at the hotel later that afternoon so that we could view the silver stored in his flat. Fortunately, my Polish was good enough to communicate with the reticent Ukrainian.

The favourable weather prompted me to suggest visiting *Dziadzio*'s grave in the Łyczakowski Cemetery, itself a tourist destination. The three of us decided to experience the local transport and took a tram to the cemetery. I was sad to discover that, since my previous visits, the gravestone had deteriorated; the stone base was collapsing, and the stone cross was broken. Adam and I discussed how we could get it restored. We then made our way to the Armenian Cathedral so that I could show Louise and Adam with pride the de Rosen murals depicting *Strij* Andrzej.

Later that afternoon, a dishevelled Roman met us in the hotel lobby and escorted us to his flat some ten minutes' walk away, where he lived with his aged mother. I was expecting the silver to be stored discreetly in some locked cupboard, but to my surprise he led us to a spare room crammed with an extraordinary assortment of objects ranging from pot plants, cabbages and homemade vodka to bits of furniture and an assortment of bric-a-brac. There was no room to swing a cat, let alone sort any of the silver, which was still in our bags stuffed under a table in the middle of the room. There was hardly a place to sit, but I cleared a chair for myself, while Louise found a spot on the floor and Adam remained standing.

This was my first contact with the silver since hurriedly leaving Alina's flat three months previously. I gently fingered some of the smaller pieces and cast an admiring eye on the large silver platter. We did some initial sorting and put a number of damaged items aside. Then we called Roman, who was having tea in the kitchen with his mother. He had previously suggested selling the hoard to an antique dealer to whom he'd shown one or two pieces. I, of course, would have none of that, but we did end up taking a bag of broken items to the dealer in the old town. This portly fellow, who was wearing a Norwegian reindeer sweater, examined the items closely with a loupe. He must have sensed that there was more, that these bits and pieces were part of a larger collection, and politely told us that he would not be able to repair the items but would be happy to pay for them by weight. They turned out to weigh about 5 kilograms, for which I was paid in euros. I also bought a few cheap coins and medallions with a view to presenting the receipts to officials in case I was apprehended at the Ukrainian–Polish border with the items. The antiquarian seemed agreeable, as perhaps there was an expectation we would return with more interesting, undamaged pieces.

The coffee and cake shop adjacent to the George Hotel became our war room. It was there, fortified by cappuccinos, chocolate nut cake and my favourite *ciasteczka migdałowe* (almond cakes), that Louise, Adam and I strategised about ways to spirit the recovered family silver out of the country. I wondered whether the spirits of our ancestors might guide us.

Adam suggested a possibility: he had a Polish-French friend who, in turn, had a Polish friend, Jerzy, who lived in Lwów and travelled to Poland from time to time. Perhaps Jerzy could take the items piece by piece to Poland. Adam arranged to meet Jerzy, who seemed reluctant but insisted that we meet his aged mother for tea. After a few tram stops and a long cold walk through muddy streets, we duly arrived and were treated to a proper meal with much talk about the difficulties of life for Poles, who were now a minority in the town. It gave us a wonderful insight into how the locals lived, but the connection led to nothing.

In the meantime, my cousin Paweł's daughter Ewa, back in Poland, had also been racking her brains, as had her husband, Gabriel. They had befriended a Ukrainian who lived in Kyiv but regularly travelled to Poland in a large truck, as he was in the business of setting up the infrastructure for various festivals and fêtes held there from time to time. He would be willing, they told me, to transport the hoard in his truck. But Kyiv is a long distance from Lviv, and the plan would necessitate an unwieldy detour. I discussed the possibility of the driver collecting the silver in Lviv en route to Poland, but he was not particularly keen, and this would in any event compromise Roman should things go awry.

While keeping this option on the back burner, we decided to get in touch with Jendrzieowicz's contact, *Pani* Halina, the owner of the palazzo. At the very least, we'd possibly meet an interesting local, and at best she might be willing to store the silver for us. Little did I know that this would be a turning point in our mission. It had snowed the previous evening, and we made our way gingerly across the slippery paths of the large park adjoining the Ivan Franko National University of Lviv.

On arrival at the once opulent but now ageing palazzo, the three of us were escorted to *Pani* Halina's kitchen, apparently the locale where important things happen, whether one is in Lviv or Cape Town. Immediately after exchanging customary pleasantries and comments about the beautiful house, its paintings and furnishings, to my amazement *Pani* Halina asked if were related to Adam Glazewski.

'Of course, he is our grandfather!' we sang out in unison. 'How come you know of him?'

She explained that she was still involved in the campaign on behalf of the St Mary Magdalene church, which *Dziadzio* had supported some fifty years previously. Once the church had been under pressure from the communist regime; now, *Pani* Halina explained, the city wanted to use it for concerts as the church has the best pipe organ in town. I later learned that the City of Lviv had expropriated the church around the time of *Dziadzio*'s death, but the political fight to reclaim it is ongoing. *Pani* Halina told us that the dispute with the city had recently gone as far as the European Court of Human Rights in Strasbourg. I assumed this was on the grounds that the church's right to religious freedom had been violated.

Adam then announced that his daughter, Anna, had completed a master's degree in human rights the previous year in France, and had started her practical training that very month at Strasbourg, the home of the court. In my enthusiasm and excitement I rather rashly promised that Anna would more than likely be able to assist with the case. A few months later she did indeed email copies of the court papers to Adam, who forwarded them to me. Because they were in Ukrainian, I approached a Russian woman in the Cape to translate them for me, but I have not, as yet, taken the matter further.

Our animated conversation started with tea and cake in the kitchen, followed by homemade Polish vodka, which *Pani* Halina hauled out of the top shelf of her kitchen cupboard, under the genial gaze of a calendar poster of Pope John Paul II.

Adam moved the conversation to the point on hand, eventually announcing: 'Jan is here to retrieve some family heirlooms from *Dziadzio*'s estate.'

'Oh, why not talk to the Polish consulate to see if they can assist?' said *Pani* Halina.

I was not particularly excited, as I'd already emailed the distantly related official at the Polish embassy in Kyiv, who had not deigned to reply.

'One of the staff of the Polish consulate lives nearby. I'll give her a ring,' she continued.

After twenty minutes, during which time we took up an offer of a second glass of homemade vodka, *Pani* Marysia joined us in the kitchen. 'No problem,' she said. 'I'll fix an appointment tomorrow.'

The next day we took a taxi to the consulate, and on the way I said to Adam, 'What are we going to talk to the consulate people about?'

But he did not have a clear answer.

*

On arrival at the consulate we are ushered into a large book-lined boardroom where we await the official. He arrives and introduces himself. Adam does likewise, then leads the conversation, telling Zbigniew (whom we later rename Zbig) about our family background: that his father had settled in France after the war, while mine chose South Africa. Within five minutes it turns out that Zbig has recently had dinner with an in-law of Ewa's during one of his fortnightly visits to Poland. These are the same people that Louise and I had Sunday lunch with after attending Mass with Ewa and her family. The family credentials are firmly established. Once again, I note that the strong pre-war networks are still in existence. Then Adam says rather casually, 'Jan is here to repatriate or relocate some family treasure.'

'Oh yes?' replies Zbig, seemingly only partly interested.

'Our grandfather owned a manor house and buried the family treasure at the onset of World War II,' Adam continues. 'Jan dug it up recently, but it is still here in Lwów.'

'What?' The official's eyes widen with sudden interest.

'Yes,' Adam continues, 'there is, in fact, a whole lot of silver, including medallions and coins.'

I see that Zbig is now truly interested. I get up from my chair and sidle up to him, mobile phone in hand, and start showing him some of the photographs.

'Wow!' he exclaims. When he sees the two old rusty sabres, he cries out, 'I collect sabres!'

I tell him that I'd left the sabres behind with Taras. Apart from their bulk, I did not want to be carrying this incriminating evidence around. I rashly tell him that it will be no problem to get them back from Taras, though in the back of my mind I am not sure that Taras still has them or whether he will even talk to me after our previous exchange.

'I can possibly help you,' says Zbig.

We have no idea how he can help but are buoyed by his suggestion.

We leave, excited at this prospect, and agree that Zbig will come to our hotel room that evening to see the goods. Louise then goes about sorting and neatly wrapping the items in tissue paper and chalk. When they are spread out on the bed, it looks as if we have a stash of drugs. Early the next day we head off to the local market and buy three zip-up bags. They are an exact replica of the bags that are typically seen on the roofs of buses headed for rural Transkei over holiday periods. Made in China, no doubt.

We pack the hoard and take it to the downstairs lobby, hoping that the clanking sound does not attract the attention of porters and security guards. A silver SUV arrives and the official's flunkey loads the bags in the back. The three of us stand and watch as the vehicle drives off. Mission accomplished? I think to myself with some apprehension. A few weeks later I get the much-awaited WhatsApp from cousin Ewa in Poland, 'The eagle has landed.' I breathe a sigh of relief.

This was January 2020, shortly before lockdown, and were it not for Louise's persistence, the treasure would still be under lock and key in a stranger's flat in remote Ukraine. For now, at least, it is safely stowed in Poland, the country where, I believe, it rightfully belongs.

Epilogue

A FEW weeks after our return to our Cape Town home in January 2020, Louise was scheduled to go on an architectural tour to India led by one of her retired architectural professors. I had previously accompanied Louise on a similar fascinating tour to Japan and felt proficient in Japanese Architecture 101. But now I was emotionally exhausted and did not fancy the rigours of travelling in India. I dropped Louise off at the airport and headed straight to McGregor with our dogs, Rolo and Smartie.

The drive to McGregor on the N1 takes over two hours, and as I left the big city and approached the majestic Du Toitskloof mountains, my mind wandered, recalling a visit I'd paid many years previously to see 'the Angel Lady', a mystic based in Observatory, Cape Town. I told her about my career, how it had kept me going for decades, though I was now feeling tired and burned out. As the session drew to a close, she suggested that I select a card from a brightly coloured pack which she unwrapped from a silk cloth and spread face down on her table. I took a card and read aloud: 'Go to the country!' This resonated with me strongly. The opening stanzas of WB Yeats's poem 'The Lake Isle of Innisfree' came to mind:

> I will arise and go now, and go to Innisfree,
> And a small cabin build there, of clay and wattles made:

> Nine bean-rows will I have there, a hive for the honey-bee;
> And live alone in the bee-loud glade…

My reverie in the car continued. I thought also of the time I was recuperating at home from my first ankle operation early in the new millennium, when Jane Banks, my pottery friend, phoned to tell me that there was a field in McGregor which was being subdivided into sizeable plots, and that I might be interested in buying one of them. I had rushed there as soon as my new ankle allowed me to and surveyed the terrain.

An immediate attraction was that the field, in which the original thatch house still stood, lay directly behind Temenos, a spiritual retreat centre established in the mid-1990s by Billy Kennedy, who continues to lead it to this day. I had originally come to McGregor some thirty years previously to attend a residential pottery course with Jane, but I was also drawn to Temenos. Billy's vision inspired the development of a verdant garden adorned with various objects representing different religions, including Christianity, Buddhism and Judaism. He also spearheaded the establishment of the annual McGregor poetry festival, which attracts a diversity of aspirant and established poets from all over the country. To this day I gain much spiritual satisfaction from the regular Sunday morning meditation sessions at Temenos as well as attend qi gong sessions on a Tuesday morning under the watchful gaze of a large benign Buddha statue and the paradise flycatchers that nest in the branches above.

In 2012, Louise and I were married on a showery October day interspersed with bouts of sunshine in the Temenos library. Billy led an eclectic ceremony that was enjoyed by numerous family and friends. Happily our mothers, who were then both in their nineties, were there for the joyful occasion. After years of being single, I was now happily married.

The field that Jane had originally drawn my attention to was divided into twelve plots around the perimeter, with the central area being designated a private communal garden for the use of the twelve property owners. The field sloped gently down from Van Reenen to Bree streets, and I was pleased to find that, while the plots on Bree had been sold, the north-facing ones on Van Reenen, with their magnificent views of the distant Langeberg mountains, were still available. I immediately put in an offer for a plot on Van Reenen, imagining myself building a simple U-shaped house on the property and sitting smoking my retirement pipe as I contemplated the view that stretches into the distance.

It was a few years later that I met Louise, who is an architect. She drew up plans converting my 'U' concept to an 'H', resulting in a more spacious home while maintaining the idea of a stoep facing the mountains. I commissioned a personable local builder to construct the thatched-roof house under Louise's supervision, using locally made clay bricks and reclaimed window frames as well as inside doors made from yellowwood planks. This prompted a friend to inquire when we had had the house renovated.

The house was not quite completed on our wedding day. While the celebration itself was at Temenos, followed by a delectable lunch, the evening after-party was held at our house. We enjoyed dancing till the early hours before collapsing on a mattress on the bedroom floor.

At the time of our wedding, Louise and I were both still working in Cape Town, though my sights were already set on rural McGregor. I was still six years away from retiring and contemplated taking early retirement, but I am happy that I chose to hang in at UCT, for not only has my career been satisfying, but it was also a life raft during my many low periods.

On our frequent weekend visits to McGregor, Louise and I set about establishing a garden, planting local water-wise plants such as aloes and vygies. Louise was at the apex of her career, having also qualified as a heritage practitioner, and being heavily involved in the politics of development in Newlands Village, where she owned a house. We lived there, but I would often go to McGregor on my own, particularly during 2018 and 2019, the first two years of my retirement, as Louise was invariably steeped in work-related projects or else spent time with her elderly mother.

With funds I inherited from Mom, I bought a second plot abutting the communal garden but immediately opposite our own home. This would protect our magnificent view stretching across the garden to the distant Langeberg mountains. Motivated by Layla, who assists rural communities to develop vegetable gardens, we decided to create a garden together. She remarked that this would be a place for us to smell the red earth and feel my father, her grandfather, beside us. She had timed her visit to coincide with the annual McGregor poetry festival. While we worked the soil during the day, we attended poetry readings in the evening.

I coined the term 'the bottom ground' to refer to the garden, just as my father once had at Vygeboom. With the toiling in the earth, our uncle–niece relationship deepened and began to pave the way for further earth digging later together. As an aspirant gardener I became aware of how intricately we are connected to our surroundings: watching for rain, peering into my artichokes and eagerly awaiting the first harvest, seeking out seasonal seeds, and feeling the heat of the sun on my back. Working the earth brought me closer to my father, though I regretted I had not worked much with him on his 'bottom ground'. But toiling with Layla reignited the flame of returning to his Ukraine farm and touching the soil where he once worked.

*

On 23 March 2020, President Ramaphosa announced a three-week lockdown: Covid had arrived in South Africa. The day before the announcement, I supervised the harvesting of 115 kilograms of olives from the communal garden's olive grove, and also planted the first garlic plants in my vegetable plot, which I had by then established with the help of Layla.

Louise was in Cape Town when the lockdown was announced. She took up my suggestion that she come to McGregor for the three-week period, rather than my returning to her home in Newlands Village. She packed up the consumables, her computer and her files and headed for McGregor. How naive I was to imagine that the lockdown would be over soon!

My initial reaction to Covid was rather cavalier. After all, I had survived the height of the AIDS epidemic in the mid-1990s. I observed with quiet amusement how the whole world panicked, recollecting how gay men and many HIV-positive haemophiliacs had been marginalised during the height of the epidemic nearly forty years earlier. There were several upsides to living in the small community of McGregor during the lockdown. One of these was that we were fortunate to have access to the huge communal garden space. I figured out that if I walked around it three times, I would cover the distance of a kilometre. If I'd been in Louise's small Newlands home, situated on a busy road, I'd have gone out of my mind. A further advantage was that my old friends Paul and June had built a home, designed by Louise, on the land adjacent to my vegetable plot. During the isolation of lockdown we'd quietly walk over to each other's house and pass meals over the fence on alternate days. (Later, they would acquire a nearby farm with a 25-metre enclosed heated pool, allowing a number of us to swim regularly – the optimal form of exercise for a haemophiliac.)

The biggest bonus of lockdown in McGregor was Louise having the opportunity to enjoy the country lifestyle. She became involved in my vegetable gardening in between her dwindling work activities. It was a new experience to be living with Louise 24 hours a day, without her spending at least some of the time at work. She is a bundle of energy operating in top gear, while I plod along in first. She enthusiastically set about adjusting the garden layout, advising on the irrigation system, while continuing her architectural and heritage practice online and occasionally seeing clients in Cape Town. Subsequently, she has rented out her Newlands house and now lives permanently in our rural home.

During lockdown, with some adjustments, I was able to continue my daily morning amble from our house, through the communal garden, to my vegetable plot to inspect my vegetables and enjoy the satisfaction of seeing them grow. A minor inconvenience was that I was restricted from exiting from the bottom gate on to Bree Street, where I would usually continue my morning walk around the block with our two dogs. Nor could I consult with our loyal gardener Attie, who assists me in the garden, as he was confined to his home in the Ou Dorp. Fortunately, he had helped plant my first garlic crop literally the week the lockdown was announced.

I found solace in my then ageing walking companion, Rolo, who subsequently died, as I invariably contemplated the devastating effects of the virus on all our lives. In my particular case, lockdown prevented me from returning to Poland to sort through the silver in a leisurely manner and decide what to do with it, though this is, of course, a relatively minor problem. I am fully aware of how privileged I am to be able to occupy this beautiful space in a country where few enjoy such pleasures.

I have found, since being in McGregor, that I walk taller, thinking about my father and about finding the silver, realising that I have adopted more and more of his habits and routines. Like him, after my early morning stroll with the dog, I take a walk to my own 'bottom ground', check the vegetables, and come back to enjoy breakfast with Louise. While my father farmed battery chickens commercially, I simply have four free-range chickens. I scratch their backs, feed them meal supplemented by freshly picked spinach from my vegetable garden, and generally collect four eggs as 'rent' daily.

Epilogue

I remember how, during my youth and early adult years, my father would get up at dawn, come winter or summer, every day of the week except Sundays, and head to his 'bottom ground' at Vygeboom. He would have his handful of workers harvest the vegetables and take the fresh produce to the old farmstall on Durbanville Avenue. I regret that I did not spend more time with him on his vegetable patch, where he also grew globe artichokes, as I now also do, getting much satisfaction from introducing them to family and friends.

When going down to the local shop, I often encounter smiling faces and friendly greetings. 'Oom Jan!' young and old voices call out to me. Interacting with the local community in McGregor takes me back to my childhood days on Cotswold farm with my immediate friends Korrie, Dawie and Sydney. I see their faces in the groups of young boys whose fathers are often absent and who are in need of kindness and attention.

But the village is by no means idyllic. In many ways it is a microcosm of South Africa, where the gap between rich and poor is all too evident and discomforting. A block away from our paradise garden is White City, a recently constructed social housing scheme to accommodate people previously living in shacks or workers relocated from neighbouring farms. From a distance the settlement looks like a shimmering Greek village, but closer inspection reveals people living in overcrowded conditions and poverty. Neighbouring farms are being mechanised and work is seasonal in the district. There is no manufacturing or similar activity to provide employment. In winter, while I light my fireplace, I hear kids dragging branches on the road from the scrubland on the other side of the village, which they take home for fire. Ragged barefoot children come to the door asking for food. Why aren't they at school where there is a regular feeding scheme? I learn that since Covid, when schooldays were curtailed, children see no point in returning to classes.

*

I frequently ponder some of the parallels between my father's new life in Durbanville and my own in McGregor. Like him, I grow vegetables; like him, I adhere to farming routines; like him, I have an amicable relationship with the people who work in my garden; like him, I live in the midst of a poor community with whom I enjoy a mutually respectful relationship.

But, unlike my father, I am fortunate not to have been forced out of the country of my birth, a country that has given me wealth beyond silver. I have enjoyed the privilege of a platinum education and world-class medical care. I have lived a long and rich life, in spite of numerous medical problems, while so many in the same boat have not. For this, I am grateful beyond words.

Yet now, as I complete this memoir, some two years after retrieving the family treasure from Ukraine, my seemingly idyllic McGregor life has been shattered: Ukraine has been invaded by its Slavic Russian brothers. I am outraged and profoundly concerned. My first thought was that the war would be limited to the Donbas region in eastern Ukraine, a region of combat for a number of years as Vladimir Putin attempts to gain a land bridge to Crimea, practically without resistance or condemnation from the West, which he unlawfully annexed during Barack Obama's presidency.

I therefore assumed that my ancestral hometown, Lviv, far to the west, would remain unscathed. But it soon became clear that Putin has set his sights on a much larger area, including the capital, Kyiv, which suffered a barrage of missile attacks. It turned out that I was wrong about only the east being under siege. I was unnerved to hear reports that a munitions depot on the outskirts of Lviv had been attacked. Later I learned that a missile had fallen near Ivano-Frankivsk, where Taras, our metal detector man, lives. I contacted him via Messenger and was relieved to learn that he was okay.

I watch events unfold daily on the BBC and am appalled by the accounts of atrocities committed against innocent civilians, including

Epilogue

women and children. I am riveted by images of refugees crowding the picturesque Lviv station. It was virtually deserted when, not so long ago, I was there, and I remember, as my train approached, a panicky fellow traveller rummaging in his shabby bag for his ticket. Now there are thousands of frightened people waiting on the platforms to leave.

The Russian invasion prompts me to revisit my father's mini-memoir. Then, as now, refugees were streaming into Romania, which, at that time, bordered Poland. In my father's words, 'There was still a stream of Poles leaving illegally Poland into Romania.' It strikes me that Romania then played a similar role to that of Poland today. I am happy that, in the current crisis, the Poles have generously opened their arms to assist fleeing fellow Slavs, but I can't help remembering how, only a few years ago, Poland closed its borders to fleeing Syrians and others making their way to Europe from the war-torn Middle East.

My father's account continues: 'After the war, the peasants from Chmielowa, who were mostly Ruthenians, and who were by the Russians considered Ukrainians, were deported into Siberia. The Polish peasants were resettled into the western part of Poland near Wrocław where the Germans were evacuated.'

I close the unfinished memoir and look out of my window at the tranquil surrounds of our garden. I fall into a reverie. How fortunate my parents and their offspring were to have avoided the forced deportations of their countrymen to Russia and Belarus. But what fate, I wonder, will befall today's fleeing Ukrainians? I note that the region has suffered atrocities under successive waves of invaders and the Holocaust. I wonder what memorials will be erected in years to come after this war has ended in Lviv and other Ukrainian cities to mark the current atrocities. It is comforting to know that I recovered the family silver when I did. It would not have been possible right now, and no one knows how long this war will last.

Epilogue

While the war rages on, I have – to draw on Yeats again – nine bean-rows and more in a place where peace has come to me, despite the glint of the remaining silver in Poland.

LAYLA'S DIARY

DAY 1

I extend a hand into the past, fingers outstretched, trying to hold on to something. How do we know this is all real? We stand on the shoulders of those who came before us, seeing further than we could do so by ourselves. Slowly we move away. I carry up the hill a sack of pure silver that eighty years previously my grandfather carried down on the same path, anxious and hurried. I am there and here: we share these objects and this place. I feel the past now, the blurring of time; I hold it softly in my hands.

Today we got lost twice: a woman with wild hair, a sixteen-year-old with a mind wide open, a man with a searching heart and a down-turned mouth, and a young, hard-footed woman. But we reached our destination in the end: a small village to the north of the Dniester River. The river winds through thick forests fading skywards and coloured with a palette of yellows and reds; autumn brings icy winds and fire colours. The land is high up, overlooking the river and a hamlet across the way. It's covered in rosehip, yarrow, thistle and ruins. The forest lies thick and whispering to the west and far to the east.

On arrival we meet an archaeologist and produce our tattered map. Immediately it is apparent my uncle is not as prepared as he would have liked. He hasn't been to Chmielowa farm in eight years. His first comment is, 'I cannot believe everything has grown so much. How will we find the foundations of the farmhouse?' He has forgotten that the world grows while he rests in the past.

Two wars have ravaged this area, a revolution has swept through, and the many scars on the earth's surface show evidence of local people searching for their own fortunes. I move ahead of the group, and feel a breath of relief as I walk between old trees with birds filling the spaces beside me. The air is fresh and burns my nose. I find what may be the foundations of the farmhouse. They have been excavated recently but are unreadable. After an hour of searching for ancient stone walls that have left no trace at all, we follow the wavy line on the map to the edge of the forest. My grandfather wrote, 'On the left side of the pencil drawn map you will see the broken line going from the stone wall towards the forest (oaks) it is there on the border of the forest but already among the trees that you must look for our silver and my hunting guns.'

The forest is dense. I kick up leaves, looking at the forest margin, asking the land for clues as to how much it has grown in eighty years. Which oaks does my grandfather speak of? My uncle collapses on to the sloping ground; he cannot get down as I do. Embarrassment and disappointment are beginning to replace hope in him. It is very clear we don't have enough clues to work from, and the surroundings are vast and wild. The metal detector we have with us is screaming at every step, for the soil is layered with bullet shells and broken farming equipment.

The other three disappear and I sit beside my uncle, whose watery eyes peer into the trees. A robin lands beside us and I muse that it may be his father – my grandfather. We ask it for guidance. It flies into a nearby bush and surveys us, looking somewhat disgruntled at being disturbed. I consider my love for this wild place. Perhaps my love of wilderness has been given to me as a gift from my grandfather, through my mother. The wind whips at our pink faces. My uncle's finger has been cut open on a rosehip bush and he watches it bleeding steadily. I suppress the urge to wrap him in my arms; he is proud and won't welcome my sympathy.

We agree to go back to the hotel and find a map from the 1930s. We need scale and exactness to begin our search for something that might have disappeared a long time ago. I walk the length of the farm alone while the others drink tea in the car. It is an other-worldly place. I imagine my ancestors being displaced from it and their anguish at losing everything. While I don't feel any profound connection with my grandfather, I do feel an intense closeness to my mother, who has chosen a life of appreciation for the natural world. There are yarrow flowers blooming near my feet. I sink my hands into the ground and feel the weight of my family, of what it takes to survive.

DAY 2

I'm sitting with my heels tucked beneath me, protecting my clothing from the frost that clings to the steaming ground. Leaves are falling everywhere, sunlight picking up the fire as they drift down. The edge of the forest leans towards me, pulling me in, and I have to stop myself from running with the falling leaves.

Our unlikely team meets at the hotel entrance to prepare for a second day of searching. Today we are armed with another map, pre-World War II, and are keen to talk to the local villagers to see if we can glean better memories than my uncle's, which seem to be flickering. Chmielowa in the Ternopil region is a tiny settlement, with no more than four hundred people, most of whom are elderly: the youth flee to the cities to escape rural life and find the comforts of the modern world.

We park outside the only school in the village: thirty-seven children gathered in a little building with religious images thick on the walls. Filing into the headmaster's tiny room, we sit down or stand against the pale blue walls. The principal has an open, oval face with wide, kind eyes and a fresh, dignified way about him. He is overjoyed to have visitors from a country as foreign and remote as South Africa. We ask about the farm, whether he knows any elderly people who worked there or who could point out where the buildings once stood. The farm was abandoned in 1939 with the invasion of the Russians. Next came the Germans, followed by the Soviets, who liberated and subsequently occupied the country. The farm was run as a co-operative until the Soviet Union fell and the land was then left to the local village for foraging and for cattle to graze. There are two buildings, one erected recently and one dating from when our family were the landowners. The first bit of information we learn is that the farm is referred to as the 'Polish hill' and that Adam Glazewski was a very respected landowner, despite conflict between the local Ukrainians and Polish landowners.

Speaking with an animated babble of words, the headmaster announces that he will join us on our walk into the village to speak to some of the elderly women. We follow a dusty road to a crooked blue house, with corn drying outside. The headmaster calls to the woman to come out. She is horrified, exclaiming that she is far too dirty to talk to people from the city. A second woman comes hurtling out of the neighbouring house, dusting flour from her gnarled hands and smiling through several missing teeth. These women have stepped straight out of an old tale. Headscarves hold their cheeks high, round and rosy. Their backs are curved, they stand lower than my shoulder, and their flat feet rest in thick felt slippers. Chattering, they tell stories about stories. Both were born in the 1940s and so never met the Polish landowners. They have been told many stories of the abundant farm, the grapevines that covered the hills, and the head of the family who was so good to the local people. One of the women charges off to save her baking bread from burning and returns with handfuls of freshly collected walnuts to give to us.

They send us down the street to find Paulina, the oldest woman in the village, the one with the brightest memory. We pass couples collecting huge root vegetables, which they spread out in the dappled sunlight beneath the chestnut trees. At the next house two women gesture wildly towards the hill and once again talk about how good Glazewski was, about how, after he left, they were sometimes paid only with a bunch of grapes for a full day's work. A small solitary bee hovers near my face, and I feel I breathe easier with the faint hum it emits. Paulina, Paulina, everyone repeats: we must find this elderly woman who is filled with youth. We wind down the village and arrive at her gate. A man passing by joins us in calling for her and she comes to the gate. We are greeted with a glare, her blackened hands holding tightly to a smooth walking stick. Her back is bowed, her eyes are clear, her face is etched with the lines of years. The archaeologist explains our situation, that we are trying to find the cellar of the farmhouse, asking if she can point out where the buildings once stood. She nods; she says she will come to the farm with us; she remembers everything. Jan hastily tries to photograph her, with boyish excitement in his eyes. She lifts a stained hand to shield her face from the camera. The little man who accompanied us jumps in the car too; our party has now doubled in number.

At the farm Paulina steps out of the car, declining all hands that reach out to help her. She walks evenly and steadily forward, and begins to point out where everything once had stood, painting a picture of the past. We find the cellar, huge and intact. It's a strange feeling to stand in a stone room underground, knowing that relatives you've never met stood here in a very different time. It is clear now that the map makes little sense; nothing is where it is said to be. Paulina insists on walking down the steep incline to a cross on the edge of the hill. Once more she will not accept any assistance.

She speaks softly, about the farmland that once lay here, the cherry trees, the apricots, the vineyards, the large vegetable garden. A shaking hand points to where the forest begins; she tells us this has always been where the forest stood. Every sentence ends with a voice steeped in pain, repeating the line 'There was so much and now it is all gone, everything is gone.' We ask about her own life and she talks about a life of war, never ending. She spent time in a concentration camp before the Soviets liberated it, and then returned home. 'The Russians have come, the Germans have come, and I have survived them all,' she mutters in Ukrainian. We return to the entrance and make our way towards the car. We offer to drive her home, but Paulina shakes her head, lifts a curled hand and begins a slow shuffle down the hill towards the village.

Women have now entered the fields to pick rosehips; they sneak side glances at us, wondering what we are doing ambling across their land. I study the map, trying to get inside my grandfather's mind. The garden would have needed sun, the animals would have been closer to the house, the church is in the wrong place on the map. I swivel it a few times, and when it is facing in one direction, everything makes sense except for a small arrow pointing towards the river. The arrow is the problem. I show the archaeologist what happens when I change the orientation. Jan overhears me and sheepishly admits to having added the arrow much later, and that he could have been wrong. Now we have something to work from. We start searching in a new area and slowly we begin our discovery.

The foundations of the piggery show themselves, as well as the yard walls: the dotted line on the map now has a solid starting point. The archaeologist and I are hopping about, relieved at finally finding something that will orientate us. We decide to make one more search. I use a compass to direct me to the edge of the forest. The metal detector beeps loudly at the first spot we try, and a tremble ripples through the group, now consisting of the original four. Jan sits twenty metres up beyond the tree line. We dig and uncover a strip of barbed wire. The next beep gives us large pieces of rusted metal. I step on a bone that is almost certainly human. We are digging through wars, through layers of various occupations. This solid ground, like Pauline, is testimony to things that have lasted.

After a while the search begins to feel aimless and fruitless once again. The edge of the forest stretches a long way, we are tired, the map is not to scale, having been drawn from memory fifty years after my grandfather fled from this land. A bright golden beetle lands on my arm. The trees are singing in the light, icy wind. We are searching for things of sentimental value, relics from the past, a confirmation of a story, in response to a command that a son feels he needs to follow to relieve himself of a weight on his chest that has never lifted. We sit and gaze around. It's all a tease, looking for something that may be just one shovelful of earth away. The light is fading, it's time to move on again. Jan looks deflated but accepts it is time to be on our way. We climb into the car and leave this land of hidden objects and abundant nature.

DAY 3

On 11 October, my uncle Janek and I wake up in a strange, garishly decorated hotel in a small city in the south-west of Ukraine. Neither of us slept well after an evening of half-translated conversation, dining with two men who couldn't speak much English. Today we have decided to give it one more chance. Our archaeologist friend has found a better metal detector and insists we return to the farm. We have just spent two short days holidaying in the Carpathian mountains. Our two other team members have returned to their home in Lwów, but we have come halfway across the world for this mission and we can't resist this final day of searching. At eight we meet a thick-necked, slightly off-putting Ukrainian man, an ex-student of the archaeologist. The man speaks a few words of English and can dig if we need help. His low-slung car playing terrible Russian pop music will be our chariot to the farm. The previous night his slightly chauvinist remarks and sweeping glances left me with a bitter taste in my mouth.

Two hours pass in his car, with few words spoken as we slide around corners, narrowly missing ducks, dogs and gaping holes in the road. We grind to a halt on the grassy driveway at the entrance to the farm. Imprints of our feet from a few days before mingle with fresh hoof marks. The wind is cold again, it slips into my collar and curls its fingers around my neck. We bundle together bags of tools and metal detectors and set off down a line set by the compass, swaying off slightly here and there to avoid patches of thorn and rolling ditches. The dotted line that my grandfather drew on his map hovers somewhere above our heads. We enter the forest. This time Janek struggles down the slope with us, determined not to be left behind. We dump everything on the marked spot and make a rough-and-ready decision to work fifteen metres on either side with the detectors, perhaps ten metres up and down too.

I begin my search for natural clues, old tree stumps, soil built up by moving water. I'm not convinced we are on what was the forest edge eighty years ago. The Ukrainian man refuses to let me have a turn with the smaller detector, muttering, 'No, no, no, you are girl, you no dig and no struggle.' I suppress the urge to knock him on the head with my 'girly' fist, and march off to see what the elder man has found. We look haphazardly for a while. Janek shuffles to and fro, distracted by things we can't see. The men move in opposite directions, the young one leaving his detector on the ground a second too long – long enough for me to snatch it up and move into a grove of older trees.

The archaeologist calls for me to bring the second detector over, and I start towards him. But I am intercepted by the thick-necked man who grabs the detector and makes his way forward. Frustration washes over me, and I begin to feel once again the sense of emotional separation I have felt for the past few days. Experiencing things differently from those around you can be incredibly lonely. Jan and I lean against the young oak trees, taking in the dancing shadows and soft smells. We discuss the numerous possibilities and use the same expressions about needing perhaps to move on and put this all to rest. The two men have begun to dig into the ground, and the smell of broken roots fills my nose. A memory filters into my mind of being on a cliff in southern Nepal, smelling the upturned trees as a road is ripped through the forest.

A few moments of silence pass and then comes the faintest sound, a soft knocking on a door closed many years before. It is the noise of the spade hitting something buried in the subsoil. 'A stone,' our archaeologist mutters, while continuing to dig. The sound comes again, only now it has a metallic ring to it. He looks up at us, his eyes wide in disbelief. The ground moves aside and the round shape of an upturned candlestick emerges. Janek whispers something inaudible into the electric air. Just in case his hopes are dashed again, I speculate aloud that this might not be 'our' treasure after all. I pass down a thin metal probe, which is inserted into the area around the candlestick. The muffled sounds of solid objects being struck are unmistakable: these are no stones here. We pull the candlestick out. It is slightly oxidised and bent out of shape. The younger man plunges the spade back into the ground. His pace has quickened, his eyes are narrow with excitement. The metallic strikes fill the air around us. The next candlestick is wrapped in faded newspaper whose text – in Polish – is still readable.

My uncle's body leans forward, tilting on the balls of his feet. His face resembles that of his boyhood, normally tight eyes have opened completely and are filled with tears, his mouth hangs open. The hole grows and reveals the edge of something unmistakably dazzling – perfect shining silver. We all raise our voices to urge caution: the digger is moving too fast, in too frenzied a way. I find my own voice and firmly move him aside, picking up the smaller spade to chip delicately away at the soil on either side of the silver. A jug, a platter, more candlesticks and then some more; an entire candelabrum in fact. A more vigorous move with the spade splinters the wall of the hole and splits open an almost entirely decomposed beaded bag. Coins spill on to my hands, with a sound of clinking that seems strange. We are affirmed. I wipe the soil from a thick silver coin that has my great-grandfather's name engraved on it and I notice my fingers quivering under the weight of this small object from almost a century ago. It is as if the ground has opened its mouth and is finally telling us its secrets.

Small silver boxes are opened containing broken jewellery: a shining amethyst cross, an ornately carved angel, a silver leaf, my grandfather's christening spoon. We take turns to dig. I take over when the excavation requires more intricate manoeuvres. Each time I reach for something, I am reminded that the last people to touch it were my ancestors, men who share my blood. Soon the bags we have brought are full, and the young man and I leave the trees, with sacks over our shoulders, weighed down and clinking.

We walk along the same line back to the car. My feet move swiftly up the hill, my belly tight with the tension of accomplishment and disbelief. I see my grandfather and his brothers moving down the hill towards me, their arms laden. Their four faces display similar emotions as they are forced to leave the land they love and have tended so carefully. They move silently past me, in the dusk of eighty years gone by. We have found their treasure, which they were never able to return to and recover. The weight of their displacement bound up their feelings in boxes as hard as this silver and sank heavily into their beings. In some way, those that carry their blood have returned and completed their story. We empty the silver into the car, and I feel a peculiar blurring of time while looking at the soiled relics that lie on the car boot floor.

We return to the now human-sized wound in the ground and fill the bags again and again. Strange things begin to arise, emotions of elation and accomplishment as well as of tension and angst as the hoard grows in size. The younger man becomes more aggressive; he insists on handling some of the objects first, and I resist. I feel strongly that Jan should be the one to place his hands on the fading prints of his father's fingers. But he cannot lean down to pull anything out; his weathered body won't allow it. The Ukrainian dialogue between the two men becomes strained. No one ever expected the haul to be so large. What do they want now for their part in finding it?

The earth tears deeper and reveals the barrel of one of my grandfather's hunting guns. The gun lies next to a disfigured piece of metal, now rusted and disintegrating. The guns are here, the silver is here, my grandfather's words rise up around us. We are living out a family story that has been told over and over without any expectation of an ending. I wish the silver would turn into light and pour into my uncle's astonished eyes, filling up the holes that have haunted his life.

ABOUT THE AUTHOR

JAN GLAZEWSKI ('Janek') was born in Paarl, South Africa, in 1953 to Polish immigrant parents. He was diagnosed a severe haemophiliac at birth. In 1985, the same year that he began a successful career in the Institute of Marine and Environmental Law at UCT at the age of 32, he tested positive for HIV from contaminated blood products used to treat his bleeding disorder. He was told that he would not live long and as a result did not get married until much later in life.

Despite these and other setbacks, Jan went on to have a successful environmental law career and, among other things, was involved in ensuring the incorporation of environmental rights in both the Namibian and South African constitutions. He has also written a leading textbook in the field, *Environmental Law in South Africa*, which is updated annually.

In 2019, in his first year of retirement, Jan fulfilled a lifelong dream by unearthing the family silver buried by his father 80 years previously at the onset of World War II in former Poland, now Ukraine. He used a rough sketch map drawn by his father, and was assisted by a Ukrainian metal detector man and his 28-year-old niece Layla.

Photo: Sung-Yee Tchao